AF709481

SMACK!

SMACK!

by The Editors of
RAMPARTS Magazine
and
Frank Browning

HARROW BOOKS
Harper & Row, Publishers
New York, Evanston, San Francisco, London

Some of these articles appeared previously in *Ramparts*. "Drug Law History" appears by permission of the Health Policy Advisory Center.

"The Living Death of Junkie Augie Schultz," article by Lois Wille, © 1971 Chicago Daily News. Reprinted with permission.

"The Political Economy of Junk" copyright © by Sol Yurick, 1970. First published in the *Monthly Review*, December 1970.

"Heroin in the Military" and "Interview with David Raskin" appeared previously in *Organ* Magazine, July 1971.

Copyright © 1972 by Noah's Ark, Inc.
All rights reserved. Printed in the United States of America. No part of this book may be used or reproduced in any manner without written permission except in the case of brief quotations embodied in critical articles and reviews. For information contact *Ramparts* Magazine, 2054 University Avenue, Berkeley, California. Published simultaneously in Canada by Fitzhenry & Whiteside Limited, Toronto.

First Harrow edition published 1972.

LIBRARY OF CONGRESS CATALOG CARD NUMBER: 75–187046

STANDARD BOOK NUMBER: 06–0870192

Designed by Yvette A. Vogel

Contents

Introduction

Just before the spring thaw came in February 1971, *CBS News* brought forth one of those soul and fact reports that tend to turn gourmet dining into acute gastritis. The story was smack. In itself, the fact of heroin addiction hadn't usually qualified as news material. But this story had a new twist, for the setting was lovely, green, suburban Westport, Connecticut. And the principals were not center-city toughs, but instead the Pepsi and pompon girls. Tucked behind idolatrous posters of Paul (McCartney) or beneath the ears of stuffed Snoopy dogs were the vials and the needles and other paraphernalia for maintaining a heroin habit. Lining the alabaster arms of eager would-be debutantes were the unmistakable hypodermic tracks that for generation on generation have hounded heroin addicts in America's black ghettos. A most disturbing interruption from evening mealtime enjoyment, the news report made clear what many had known for some time: that an unparalleled heroin epidemic had been loosed upon every sector of American life. Worse yet: when smack moved to the suburbs, it brought with it all the grisly details of big-time crime and hideous, painful death.

Now smack had become one of America's most pressing issues. Mayors, Congressmen, Senators, and even President Nixon himself have worked it into their campaign speeches. It is a problem of "pandemic virulence," Nixon tells us, one that requires comprehensive action. Perhaps Nixon has said more than he knows, for heroin is so comprehensive that it is in many ways metaphoric for the American way of life. To examine the structure and dimensions of the heroin problem is to examine the American polity in microcosm—to see the full extent of its exploitative empire abroad and to focus close in on the psychic and physical rape of its citizens at home.

The United States is the number one consumer of heroin in the world today, just as she is the number one consumer of the world's vital resources. Approximately $3 billion are spent annually to support her heroin habits, and the figure has grown sharply over the last decade. Senator Vance Hartke told the Congress in the spring of 1971 that there are some 500,000 Americans who use heroin. Reports coming back from Vietnam place the percentage of smack users there at anywhere from 20 to 30 percent, while officers running so-called drug amnesty centers admit they have had almost no impact at stemming the tide of addiction.

To black and brown Americans all of these findings may seem to provide a certain ironic justice. Their communities have been pacified and emaciated by smack since the turn of the century, and no one ever thought to declare any epidemics of national significance. Mobsters got rich off the trade, and police in city after city took their payoffs all along. Hence there is little surprise that nothing would be done until the depth of depravity became so great as to suck in those middle-class Americans who had always been blind to the ravages of smack. What this book attempts to do is demonstrate just how completely that depravity has permeated American society. The articles presented here by no means seek to be categorically definitive; instead the broad scope of their subject matter shows the close integration of the international traffic in heroin with America's economic and military institutions abroad and with the daily life of her citizens at home.

With two exceptions the articles are all journalistic investigations of some phase of the heroin problem. Remaining is a description of a U.S. Army drug amnesty center in South Vietnam given by the center's director, and though his speculations about the sources of opium and heroin are probably somewhat off base (that is, contrary to his own speculation, there is no evidence that the National Liberation Front forces have ever been involved in drug traffic), he gives perhaps the first direct account of how the military program completely fails to confront the problem of servicemen's drug habits. Finally we have included a special report compiled by Congressmen Morgan Murphy and Robert Steele for the House Foreign Affairs Committee. That report goes far toward substantiating *Ramparts*' own report that the United States military and its client forces in Indochina have long been directly involved in shipping drugs to American citizens and servicemen.

Combined with our own story on the Indochinese opium and heroin traffic, the Murphy and Steele report offers the plainest explanation of how American foreign policy makers have been willing to go to any extremes—even to the extreme of converting a quarter of their fighting forces in Vietnam into strung-out, haggard "scagheads"—to carry out their schemes of global conquest.

Bitter as it may seem, the conquest over American forces in Indochina by drug addiction is a fitting end to America's Vietnam adventure. For that adventure bloomed full strength out of the moral vacuum that has guided American policy makers, policy makers who threw legality and moral imperatives to the wind before the force of their military and strategic ends. *Ramparts'* most recent research has indicated there is more than a little reason to suppose that the U.S. State Department and the Central Intelligence Agency have been at least objective colleagues with international Mafiosi in the drug-pushing enterprise; however, until more conclusive data is brought forth, one may only speculate how much further that relationship leads. But whatever attendant investigation may show, there is a terrible justice in discovering that the principal produce of America's underworld—addiction to smack—has been turned back upon the sons and daughters of those policy makers who have relied upon the law of the underworld to shape America's destiny.

FRANK BROWNING

August, 1971

1. The CIA and the New Opium War

by Frank Browning and Banning Garrett

"Mr. President, the specter of heroin addiction is haunting nearly every community in the nation." With these urgent words, Senator Vance Hartke spoke up on March 2, 1971, in support of a resolution on drug control being considered in the U.S. Senate. Estimating that there are 500,000 heroin addicts in the U.S., he pointed out that nearly 20 percent of them are teen-agers. The concern of Hartke and others is not misplaced. Heroin has become the major killer of young people between eighteen and thirty-five, outpacing death from accidents, suicides, or cancer. It has also become a major cause of crime: to sustain their habits, addicts in the U.S. spend more than $15 million a day, half of it coming from the 55 percent of crime in the cities which they commit and the annual $2.5 billion worth of goods they steal.

Once safely isolated as part of the destructive

Banning Garrett is Asian editor for *Ramparts* magazine; Frank Browning is an associate editor of *Ramparts*. Reprinted from *Ramparts* (May 1971). Researchers for the report were Michael Aldrich, Adam Bennion, and Joan Medlin. Special thanks go to author Peter Scott for permission to draw on unpublished material regarding Laos and the China Lobby.

funkiness of the black ghetto, heroin has suddenly spread out into Middle America, becoming as much a part of suburbia as the Saturday barbecue. This has gained it the attention it otherwise never would have had. President Nixon himself says it is spreading with "pandemic virulence." People are becoming aware that teen-agers are shooting up at lunchtime in schools and returning to classrooms to nod the day away. But what they don't know—and what no one is telling them—is that neither the volcanic eruption of addiction in this country nor the crimes it causes would be possible without the age-old international trade in opium (from which heroin is derived), or that heroin addiction—like inflation, unemployment, and most of the other chaotic forces in American society today—is directly related to the U.S. war in Indochina.

The connection between war and opium in Asia is as old as empire itself. But the relationship has never been so symbiotic, so intricate in its networks, and so vast in its implications. Never before has the trail of tragedy been so clearly marked as in the present phase of U.S. involvement in Southeast Asia. For the international traffic in opium has expanded in lock step with the expanding U.S. military presence there, just as heroin has stalked the same young people in U.S. high schools who will also be called on to fight that war. The ironies that have accompanied the war in Vietnam since its onset are more poignant than before. At the very moment that public officials are wringing their hands over the heroin problem, Washington's own Cold War crusade, replete with clandestine activities that would seem far-fetched even in a spy novel, continues to play a major role in a process that has already rerouted the opium traffic from the Middle East to Southeast Asia and is every day opening new channels for its shipment to the U.S. At the same time the government starts crash programs to rehabilitate drug users among its young people, the young soldiers it is sending to Vietnam are getting hooked and dying of overdoses at the rate of one a day. While the President is declaring war on narcotics and on crime in the streets, he is widening the war in Laos, whose principal product is opium and which has now become the funnel for nearly half the world's supply of the narcotic, for which the U.S. is the chief consumer.

There would have been a bloodthirsty logic behind the expansion of the war into Laos if the thrust had been to seize supply centers of opium the Communists were hoarding up to spread like a deadly virus into the free world. But the Communists did not control the opium there: processing and distribution were already in the hands of the free world. Who are the principals of this new opium war? The ubiquitous CIA, whose role in getting the U.S. into Vietnam is well known but whose pivotal position in the opium trade is not; and a rogues' gallery of organizations and people—from an opium army subsidized by the Nationalist Chinese to such familiar names as Madame Nhu and Vice President

Nguyen Cao Ky—who are the creations of U.S. policy in that part of the world.

The story of opium in Southeast Asia is a strange one at every turn. But the conclusion is known in advance: this war has come home again—in a silky gray powder that goes from a syringe into America's mainline.

Most of the opium in Southeast Asia is grown in a region known as the Fertile Triangle, an area covering northwestern Burma, northern Thailand, and Laos. It is a mountainous jungle inhabited by tigers, elephants, and some of the most poisonous snakes in the world. The source of the opium that shares the area with these exotic animals is the poppy, and the main growers are the Meo hill tribespeople who inhabit the region. The Meo men chop back the forests in the wet season so that the crop can be planted in August and September. Poppies produce red, white, or purple blossoms between January and March, and when the blossom withers, an egg-sized pod is left. The women harvest the crop and make a small incision in the pod with a three-bladed knife. The pod exudes a white latex-like substance, which is left to accumulate and thicken for a day or two. Then it is carefully gathered, boiled to remove gross impurities, and the sticky substance is rolled into balls weighing several pounds. A fraction of the opium remains to be smoked by the villagers, but most is sold in nearby rendezvous with the local smugglers. It is the Meos' only cash crop. The hill tribe growers can collect as much as $50 per kilo, paid in gold, silver, various commodities, or local currency. The same kilo will bring $200 in Saigon and $2,000 in San Francisco.

There are hundreds of routes, and certainly as many methods of transport by which the smugglers ship opium—some of it already refined into heroin—through and out of Southeast Asia. But there are three major networks. Some of the opium from Burma and northern Thailand moves into Bangkok, then to Singapore and Hong Kong, then via military aircraft, either directly or through Taiwan, to the United States. The second, and probably major, route is from Burma or Laos to Saigon or to ocean drops in the Gulf of Siam; then it goes either through the Middle East and Marseilles to the U.S. or through Hong Kong and Singapore to the West Coast. A final route runs directly from outposts held by Nationalist Chinese troops in Thailand to Taiwan and then to the U.S. by a variety of means.

One of the most successful of the opium entrepreneurs who travel these routes, a *Time* reporter wrote in 1967, is Chan Chi-foo, a half-Chinese, half-Shan (Burmese) modern-day warlord who might have stepped out of a Joseph Conrad adventure yarn. Chan is a soft-spoken, mild-mannered man in his late thirties who, it is said, is totally ruthless. He has tremendous knowledge of the geography and people of northwestern Burma and is said to move easily among them, conversing in several dialects. Yet he is also able to deal comfortably with the bankers and other businessmen who finance his operations from such centers as Bangkok and Vientiane. Under Chan Chi-foo's command are from 1,000 to 2,000 well-armed men, with the feudal hierarchy spreading down to encompass another 3,000 hill tribesmen, porters, hunters, and opium growers who pay him fealty and whom he regards about the same as the more than 500 small mules he uses for transport.

Moving the opium from Burma to Thailand or Laos is a big and dangerous operation. One of Chan's caravans, says one awe-struck observer, may stretch in single file for well over a mile, and may include 200 mules, 200 porters, 200 cooks and camp attendants, and about 400 armed guards. Such a caravan can easily carry 15 to 20 tons of opium, worth nearly a million dollars when delivered to syndicate men in Laos or Thailand.

To get his caravans to market, however, Chan must pay a price, for the crucial part of his route is heavily patrolled not by Thais or Laotians but by nomadic Nationalist Chinese or Kuomintang (KMT) troops. Still supported by the ruling KMT on Taiwan, Generalissimo Chiang Kai-shek's 93d Division controls a major part of the opium flowing out of Burma and Thailand. Roving bands of mercenary bandits, they fled to northern Burma in 1949 as Chiang's armies were being routed on the Chinese mainland, and have maintained themselves since by buying opium from the nearby Meo tribesmen which they then resell, or by exacting tribute payments from entrepreneurs like Chan Chi-foo. As travelers to the area attest, these troops also supplement their income by running Intelligence operations into China and Burma for the U.S.

The Burmese government regularly complained about all this activity to the United Nations, the Taiwan government, and the United States, charging the Americans and Taiwanese with actively supplying and supporting the KMT, which in turn has organized antigovernment guerrillas. In 1959 Burmese ground troops seized three opium-processing plants set up by the KMT guerrillas at Wanton; the troops also took an airstrip the Chinese had used to fly in reinforcements. By February 1961 the Burmese had pushed the KMT troops southeast into the Thai-Burmese and Thai-Laotian border areas, where they now hold at least eight village bases. Just last year a reporter was at Chieng Mai, Thailand, saw Thai troops and American advisers as well as military supplies provided by the Taiwan government. The Taiwan government, he noted, maintains an information office there and regularly accompanies the KMT troops on their forays into China to proselytize among the peasants of Yünnan province. These sorties are coordinated by the CIA (which is feverishly active if not wholly successful in this area), and the United States even provides its own backwater R&R for the weary KMT, flying its helicopters from hilltop to hilltop to pick up the Chinese (and the Establishment reporter who supplied this information) for organized basketball tournaments.

Although the KMT troops are often referred to

as "remnants," they are not just debris left behind by history. They are in fact an important link in American and Taiwan policy toward Communist China. Not only does Chiang Kai-shek maintain direct contact with his old 93d, but fresh recruits are frequently sent to maintain a troop level of from 5,000 to 7,000 men, according to a top-ranking foreign aid official in the U.S. government. And, as the *New York Times* has noted, Chiang Kai-shek's son, Chiang Ching-Kuo, is widely believed to be in charge of the KMT operations from his position as chief of the Taiwan secret police.

The KMT are tolerated by the Thais for several reasons: they have helped in the counterinsurgency efforts of the Thai and U.S. governments against the hill tribespeople in Thailand; they have aided the training and recruiting of Burmese guerrilla armies for the CIA; and they offer a payoff to the Border Patrol Police (BPP), and through them to the second most powerful man in Thailand, Minister of the Interior General Prapasx Charusathira. The BPP were trained in the fifties by the CIA and now are financed and advised by AID and are flown from border village to border village by Air America. The BPP act as middlemen in the opium trade between the KMT in the remote regions of Thailand and the Chinese merchants of Bangkok. These relationships, of course, are flexible and changing, with each group wanting to maximize profits and minimize antagonisms and dangers. But the established routes vary, and sometimes double crosses are intentional.

In the summer of 1967 Chan Chi-foo set out from Burma through the KMT's territory with 300 men and 200 packhorses carrying nine tons of opium, with no intention of paying the usual fee of $80,000 protection money. But troops cut off the group near the Laotian village of Ban Houei Sai in an ambush that turned into a pitched battle. Neither group, however, had counted on the involvement of the kingpin of the area's opium trade: the CIA-backed Royal Lao government army and air force, under the command of General Ouane Rathikoune. Hearing of the skirmish, the general pulled his armed forces out of the Plain of Jars in northeastern Laos, where they were supposed to be fighting the Pathet Lao guerrillas, and engaged two companies and his entire air force in a battle of extermination against both sides. The result was nearly 30 KMT and Burmese dead and a half-ton windfall of opium for the Royal Lao government.

In a moment of revealing frankness shortly after the battle, General Rathikoune, far from denying the role that opium had played, told several reporters that the opium trade was "not bad for Laos." The trade provides cash income for the Meo hill tribes, he argued, who would otherwise be penniless and therefore a threat to Laos' political stability. He also argued that the trade gives the Lao elite (which includes government officials) a chance to accumulate capital to ultimately invest in legitimate enterprises, thus building up Laos' economy. But if these rationalizations seemed weak, far less convincing was the general's assertion that, since he is in total control of the trade now, when the time comes to put an end to it he will simply put an end to it.

It is unlikely that Rathikoune, one of the chief warlords of the opium dynasty, will decide to end the trade soon. Right outside the village of Ban Houei Sai, hidden in the jungle, are several of his refineries—called "cookers"—which manufacture crude morphine (which is refined into heroin at a later transport point) under the supervision of professional pharmacists imported from Bangkok. Rathikoune also has "cookers" in the nearby villages of Ban Khwan, Phan Phung, and Ban Kheung (the latter for opium grown by the Yao tribe). Most of the opium he procures comes from Burma in caravans such as Chan Chi-foo's; the rest comes from Thailand or from the hill tribespeople (Meo and Yao) in the area near Ban Houei Sai. Rathikoune flies the dope from the Ban Houei Sai area to Luang Prabang, the Royalist capital, in helicopters given by the United States military aid program.

Others in the Lao elite and government own refineries. There are cookers for heroin in Vientiane, two blocks from the king's residence; near Luang Prabang; on Khong Island in the Mekong River on the Lao-Cambodian border; and one recently built by Kouprasith Abhay (head of the military region around Vientiane, but also from the powerful Abhay family of Khong Island) at Phou Khao Khouai, just north of Vientiane. Other Lords of the Trade are Prince Boun Oum of Southern Laos, and the Sananikone family, called the "Rockefellers of Laos." Phoui Sananikone, the clan patriarch, headed a U.S.-backed coup in 1959 and is presently president of the National Assembly. Two other Sananikones are deputies in the Assembly, two are generals (one is chief of staff for Rathikoune), one is minister of public works, and a host of others are to be found at lower levels of the political, military, and civil service structure. And the Sananikones' airline, Veha Akhat, leases planes and pilots from Taiwan for paramilitary operations which lend themselves easily to commerce with opium-growing tribespeople. But the opium trade is popular with the rest of the elite, who rent RLG aircraft or create fly-by-night airlines (such as Laos Air Charter or Lao United Airlines) to do their own direct dealing.

Control of the opium trade has not always been in the hands of the Lao elite, although the U.S. has been at least peripherally involved in who the beneficiaries were since John Foster Dulles' famous 1954 commitment to maintain an anti-Communist Laos. The major source of the opium in Laos has always been the Meo growers, who were selected by the CIA as its counterinsurgency bulwark against the Pathet Lao guerrillas. The Meos' mountain bastion is Long Cheng, a secret base 80 miles northeast of Vientiane, built by the CIA during the 1962 Geneva Accords period. By 1964 Long Cheng's population was nearly 50,000, comprised largely of refugees who had come to escape the war and who were kept busy growing poppies in the hills surrounding the base.

The secrecy surrounding Long Cheng has hidden the trade from reporters. But security has not been complete: Carl Strock reported in the January 30, 1971, *Far Eastern Economic Review:*

> Over the years eight journalists, including myself, have slipped into Long Cheng and have seen American crews loading T-28 bombers while armed CIA agents chatted with uniformed Thai soldiers and piles of raw opium stood for sale in the market (a kilo for $52). It's old hat by now, but Long Cheng is still so secret that in the past year both the U.S. embassy press attaché and the director of USAID's training center were denied clearance to visit the mountain redoubt.

The CIA not only protects the opium in Long Cheng and various other pickup points, but also gives clearance and protection to opium-laden aircraft flying out.

For some time, the primary middlemen in the opium traffic had been elements of the Corsican Mafia, identified in a 1966 United Nations report as a pivotal organization in the flow of narcotics. In a part of the world where transportation is a major problem and where air transport is a solution, the Corsicans were able to parlay their vintage World

War II airplanes (called "the butterfly fleet" or, according to "Pop" Buell, U.S. citizen-at-large in the area, "Air Opium") into a position of control. But as the Laotian civil war intensified in the period following 1963, it became increasingly difficult for the Corsicans to operate, and the Meos started to have trouble getting their crop out of the hills in safety.

The vacuum that was created was quickly filled by the Royal Lao Air Force, which began to use helicopters and planes donated by the U.S. not only for fighting the Pathet Lao but also for flying opium out from airstrips pockmarking the Laotian hills. This arrangement was politically more advantageous than prior ones, for it consolidated the interests of all the anti-Communist parties. The enfranchisement of the Lao elite gave it more of an incentive to carry on the war Dulles had committed the U.S. to back; the safe transport of the Meos' opium by an ideologically sanctioned network increased the incentive of these CIA-equipped and CIA-trained tribesmen to fight the Pathet Lao. The U.S. got parties that would cooperate with its foreign policy not only for political reasons, but on more solid economic grounds. Opium was the economic cement binding all the parties together much more closely than anti-Communism could.

As this relationship has matured, Long Cheng has become a major collection point for opium grown in Laos. CIA protégé General Vang Pao, former officer for the French colonial army and now head of the

Meo counterinsurgents, uses his U.S.-supplied helicopters and STOL (short-take-off-and-landing) aircraft to collect the opium from the surrounding area. It is unloaded and stored in hutches in Long Cheng. Some of it is sold there and flown out in Royal Laotian government C-47's to Saigon or the Gulf of Siam or the South China Sea, where it is dropped to waiting fishing boats. Some of the opium is flown to Vientiane, where it is sold to Chinese merchants who then fly it to Saigon or to the ocean drops. One of Vang Pao's main sources of transport, since the RLG Air Force is not under his control, is the CIA-created Xieng Khouang Airline, which is still supervised by an American, though it is scheduled soon to be turned over completely to Vang Pao's men. The airline's two C-47's (which can carry a maximum of 4,000 pounds) are used only for transport to Vientiane.

Prior to Nixon's blitzkrieg in Laos, the opium trade was booming. Production had grown rapidly since the early fifties to a level of 175–200 tons a year, with 400 of the 600 tons produced in Burma, and 50–100 tons of that grown in Thailand, passing through Laotian territory. But if the opium has been an El Dorado for the Corsicans, the Lao elite, the CIA, and others, it has been a nemesis for the Meo tribesmen. For in becoming a pawn in the larger strategy of the U.S., the Meos have seen the army virtually wiped out, with the average age of recruits now fifteen years, and their population reduced from 400,000 to 200,000. The Meos' reward for CIA service, in other words, has been their destruction as a people.

Both the complexity and the finality of the opium web which connects Burma, Thailand, Laos, and South Vietnam stretch the imagination. So bizarre is the opium network and so pervasive the traffic that were it to appear in an Ian Fleming plot we would pass it off as torturing the credibility of thriller fiction. But the trade is real, and the net has entangled governments beyond the steaming jungle of Indochina. In 1962, for instance, an opium-smuggling scandal stunned the entire Canadian Parliament. It was in March of that year that Prime Minister Diefenbaker confirmed rumors that nine Canadian members of the immaculate United Nations International Control Commission had been caught carrying opium from Vientiane to the international markets in Saigon on UN planes.

The route from Laos to Saigon has long been one of the well-established trails of the heroin-opium trade. In August 1967, a C-47 transport plane carrying two and a half tons of opium and some gold was forced down near Da Lat, South Vietnam, by American gunners when the pilot failed to identify himself. The plane and its precious cargo, reportedly owned by General Rathikoune's wife, were destined for a Chinese opium merchant and piloted by a former KMT pilot, L. G. Chao. Whatever their ownership, the dope-running planes usually land at Tan Son Nhut airbase, where they are met in a remote part of the airport with the protection of the airport police.

A considerable part of the opium and heroin remains in Saigon, where it is sold directly to U.S. troops or distributed to U.S. bases throughout the Vietnamese countryside. One G.I. who returned to the states an addict was August Schultz. He's off the needle now, but how he got on is most revealing. Explaining that he was "completely straight, even a right-winger" before he went into the Army, August told *Ramparts* how he fell into the heroin trap: "It was a regular day last April [1970] and I just walked into this bunker and there were these two guys shooting up. I said to them, 'What you guys doing?' Believe it or not I really didn't know. They explained it to me and asked me if I wanted to try it. I said sure."

Probably a fifth of the men in his unit have at least tried junk, August says. But the big thing, as his buddy Ronnie McSheffrey adds, was that most of the officers in his company—including the MP's—knew about it. McSheffrey saw MP's in his own division (6th Battalion, 31st Infantry, 9th Division) at Tan An shoot up, just as he says they saw him. He and his buddies even watched the unit's sergeant major receive payoffs at a nearby whorehouse where every kind of drug imaginable was available.

An article by Kansas City newspaperwoman Gloria Emerson inserted into the *Congressional Record* by Senator Stuart Symington on March 10, 1971, said:

> In a brigade headquarters at Long Binh, there were reports that heroin use in the unit had risen to 20 percent. . . . "You can salute an officer with your right hand and take a 'hit' [of heroin] in your left," an enlisted man from New York told me. . . . Along the 15-mile Bien Hoa highway running north to Saigon from Long Binh, heroin can be purchased at any of a dozen conspicuous places within a few minutes, and was by this reporter, for three dollars a vial.

Adding glamour to the labyrinthine intrigue of Vietnam's opium trade throughout the late 1950's and early 1960's was the famous Madame Nhu, the Dragon Lady of Saigon. Madame Nhu was in a position to be very likely coordinator for the entire domestic opium traffic in Vietnam; yet so great is the power she still wields from her palatial exile in Paris that she has intimidated one American publisher and kept him from publishing the story. In his book *Mr. Pop*, Don Schanche, former editor of *Horizon* and former managing editor of the *Saturday Evening Post*, recounts the following interchange on the Plain of Jars during August 1960 between Edgar "Pop" Buell—the Indiana farmer who left his home to work with the Meo tribespeople—and a local restaurateur:

> . . . Buell drove with Albert [Fouré] to Phong Savan and watched from the side of the airstrip as a modern twin-engined plane took on a huge load of opium. Beneath the wing, talking heatedly

> with the plane's Corsican pilot, was a slender woman dressed in long white silk pants and *ao d'ai*, the side-slit, high-necked gown of Vietnam. Her body was exquisitely formed, and her darkly beautiful face wore a clear expression of authority. Even Buell could see that she was Vietnamese, not Lao.
>
> "Zat," said Fouré, "is ze grande madame of opium from Saigon." Edgar never learned her name, but he recognized the unforgettable face and figure when the picture of an important South Vietnamese politician appeared months later in an American news magazine.

Though Schanche's publisher, David McKay Co., refused to publish her name for fear of reprisals, the unforgettable face was that of Madame Nhu.

But Saigon's opium trade is not new. Its history stretches back to 1949, when the French appointed former Vietnamese Emperor Bao Dai as chief of state. Bao Dai brought with him as chief of police Bay Vien, the undisputed leader of Saigon's criminal underground, which controlled not only the gambling and narcotics trade in Saigon but also the important Chinese suburb of Cholon. Bao Dai and Bay Vien held power until they were displaced after the 1954 Geneva Accords by Ngo Dinh Nhu, Diem's brother. Nhu had gained prominence in Vietnam as an organizer of a Catholic trade union movement modeled after the French Force Ouvrière, which the CIA had helped supply in the 1940's to break France's Communist dockworkers' union, the CGT.

At first Nhu feigned support for Bay Vien and Bao Dai, but by the end of 1955 he had taken control of the Saigon secret police and—thereby—the city's opium and heroin trade as well. Just as the Nhus were consolidating their own power, a little-known figure entered the Diem military apparatus—a man who through the years would carefully extend his control over the air force and end up eventually heir not only to the South Vietnamese government but to the opium and heroin trade as well. That man was Nguyen Cao Ky, who had just returned from Algeria to take charge of the South Vietnamese air transport's C-47 cargo planes.

At what particular point in time Ky became involved with the Nhus in the opium trade is not known, but by the end of the fifties he was cutting quite a figure in Saigon's elite circles. In an interview with *Ramparts,* retired Marine Corps colonel (and author of the book *The Betrayal*) William Corson described Ky's life in the late 1950's in the following fashion:

> Ky of course was a colonel in the Air Force back then and he used to have these glittering cocktail parties at the top of the Caravelle [Hotel] in Saigon. He laid out a fantastic spread—which was all very interesting because the amount of money he made as a soldier was maybe $25 to $30 a month and he didn't have any other outside income.

The first real light shed on the possible sources of Ky's extracurricular income came only in the spring of 1968, when Senator Ernest Gruening revealed that four years earlier Ky had been in the employ of the CIA's "Operation Haylift," a program which flew South Vietnamese agents "into North Vietnam for the purpose of sabotage, such as blowing up railroads, bridges, etc." More important, Ky was fired, Gruening's sources claimed, for having been caught smuggling opium from Laos back into Saigon. Significantly, Ky and his flight crews were replaced by Nationalist Chinese Air Force pilots.

Neither the CIA, the Pentagon, nor the State Department ever denied Ky worked on Operation Haylift. Nor did they deny that he had smuggled opium back into Saigon. However, a U.S. embassy spokesman categorically denied Ky was ever fired from "any position by any element of the U.S. Government for opium smuggling or for any other reason." When Ky came to power in February 1965, most observers supposed he had relinquished participation in the opium traffic (although it was "common knowledge" that Madame Ky had replaced Madame Nhu as Saigon's Dragon Lady and dealt in opium directly with Prince Boun Oum in Southern Laos). However, a high Saigon military official to whom Ky at one time offered a place in the opium traffic says Ky continued to carry loads ranging from 2,000 to 3,000 kilos of opium from Pleiku to Saigon in the spring of 1965 after he had assumed power and after Operation Haylift had been discontinued. Those runs included regular pickups near Dak To, Kon Tum, and Pleiku. Since then there has been no indication that Ky has in any way altered the transport. Corson, who returned to Vietnam in 1965, observed that Ky's involvement in the trade had become so routine that it had lost almost all its adventure and intrigue.

With gross returns from the Indochinese traffic running anywhere from $250 million to $500 million per year, opium is one of the kingpins of Southeast Asian commerce. Indochina has not always had such an enviable position. Historically most of the world's supply of opium and heroin came through well-established routes from Turkey, Iran, and China. Then it was refined in chemical kitchens and warehouse factories in Marseilles. The Mediterranean trade was controlled by the Corsican Mafia (which itself has long been related to such American crime lords as Lucky Luciano, who funneled a certain amount of dope into the black ghettos). But high officials in the narcotics control division of the Canadian government, and in Interpol, the International Police Agency, confirm that since World War II—and paralleling the U.S. expansion in the Pacific—there has been a major redirection in the sources and routing of the world-wide opium traffic.

According to the United Nations Commission on Drugs and Narcotics, since at least 1966, 80 percent of the world's 1,200 tons of illicit opium has come from Southeast Asia—directly contradicting most official U.S. claims that the primary sources are Middle Eastern. In 1966 Interpol's former secretary general Jean Nepote told investigators from Arthur D.

Little Research Institute (then under contract to the U.S. Government Crime Commission) that the Fertile Triangle was a principal production center of opium. And last year an Iranian government official told a United Nations seminar on narcotics control that 83 percent of the world's illegal supply originated in the Fertile Triangle—the area where opium is controlled by the U.S.-supplied troops of Laos and Nationalist China.

It is odd that the U.S. government, with the most massive Intelligence apparatus in history, could miss this innovation. But though it may seem to be an amazing oversight, what has happened is that Richard Nixon and the makers of America's Asian policy have completely blanked Indochina out of the world narcotics trade. Not even Joe Stalin's removal of Trotsky from the Russian history books parallels this historical reconstruction. In his recent State of the World address, Richard Nixon dealt directly with the international narcotics traffic. "Narcotics addiction has been spreading with pandemic virulence," he said, adding that "this affliction is spreading rapidly and without the slightest respect for national boundaries." What is needed is "an integrated attack on the demand for [narcotics], the supply of them, and their movement across international borders. . . . We have," he says, "worked closely with a large number of governments, particularly *Turkey*, *France*, and *Mexico*, to try to stop the illicit production and smuggling of narcotics" (italics added).

It is no accident that Nixon has ignored the real

sources of narcotics trade abroad and by so doing has effectively precluded any possibility of being able to deal with heroin at home. It is he more than anyone else who has underwritten that trade through the policies he has formulated, the alliances he has forged, and most recently the political appointments he has made. For Richard Nixon's rise to power has been intricately interwoven with the rise of proponents of America's aggressive strategy in Asia, a group of people loosely called the China Lobby who have been in or near political power off and on since 1950.

Among the most notable members of the China Lobby are Madame Anna Chennault, whose husband, General Claire Chennault, founded Air America; columnist Joe Alsop; FBI Director J. Edgar Hoover; former California Senator William Knowland; and Ray Cline, currently Chief of Intelligence for the State Department. They and such compatriots as the late *Time* magazine publisher Henry Luce and his widow, Congresswoman Claire Boothe Luce, have been some of the country's strongest proponents of the Nationalist Chinese cause.

In 1954 Chiang Kai-shek formed the Asian People's Anti-Communist League (APACL), which was to become one of the vital links between the China Lobby and the Taiwan government. (It was also in that year that Nixon urged that U.S. troops be sent into Indochina following the French defeat in Dien Bien Phu—a proposal which failed because of the lack of public support for such policy following the Korean War.) As soon as the APACL was formed,

Chiang announced that it had established "close contact" with three American politicians—the most important of whom was Vice President Richard Nixon.

Over the years the China Lobby has continued to spring to Nixon's support. It was Madame Chennault, co-chairman in 1968 of Women for Nixon-Agnew Advisory Committee, who helped raise a quarter of a million dollars for the campaign; it was she who just before the election entered into an elaborate set of arrangements to sabotage a White House peace plan. Within 30 hours of the announced plan, South Vietnam President Thieu rejected the new negotiations it proposed—a rejection Madame Chennault had helped arrange as a last-minute blow at Hubert Humphrey and the Democrats.

It is not only his debts, associations, and sympathies to the China Lobby which have linked Nixon with Kuomintang machinations in Indochina and helped plunge the U.S. deeper into the morass there. One of his most important foreign policy appointments since taking office has been the reassignment of Ray Cline as State Department director of intelligence and research. Cline, the controversial CIA station chief in Taiwan who helped organize KMT forays into Communist China, in 1962 promoted Nixon's old project of a Bay of Pigs invasion of China. Within a month of Cline's recent appointment, the resumption of pilotless Intelligence flights over mainland China was approved.

The entire cast of the China Lobby has relied on one magic corporation, the same corporation established just after World War II by General Claire Chennault as Civil Air Transport and renamed in the 1950's Air America. Carrier not only of men and personnel for all of Southeast Asia, but also of the policies that have turned Indochina into the third bloodiest battlefield in American history, Air America's chief contract is with the American Central Intelligence Agency.

Air America brings Brahmin Bostonians and wealthy Wall Streeters who are the China Lobby together with some of the most powerful men in Nationalist China's financial history. One of its principal services has been to fly in support for the "remnant" 93d Division of the KMT, the "opium army" in Burma; another has been as a major carrier of opium itself. Air America flies through all of the Laotian and Vietnamese opium pickup points, for aside from the private "butterfly fleet" and various military transports, Air America is the "official" Indochina airline. A twenty-five-year-old black man recently returned from Indochina told *Ramparts* of going to Vietnam in late 1968 as an adventurer, hoping to get in on the dope business. But he found that the business was all controlled by a "group like the Mafia. It was tight and there wasn't room for me." The only way he could make it in the dope trade, he says, was to go to work for Air America as a mechanic. He found there "was plenty of dope in Laos

—lots of crystals [heroin] all over the place." Air America was the only way to get in on it.

What has taken place in Indochina is more than a flurry of corruption among select dramatis personae in America's great Asian Drama. The fact that Meo tribesmen have been nearly wiped out, that the Corsican Mafia's Air Opium has been supplanted by the CIA's Air America, that Nationalist Chinese soldiers operate as narcotics bandits, that such architects of U.S. democracy for the East as the Nhus and Vice President Ky have been dope runners—these are only the bizarre cameo roles in a larger tragedy that involves nothing less than the uprooting of what had been *the* opium trade for decades—through the traditional lotus land of the Middle East into Western Europe—and the substitution of another network, whose shape is parallel to that of the U.S. presence in Southeast Asia. The ecology of narcotics has been disrupted and remade to coincide with the structure of America's Asia strategy—the stealthy conquest of a continent to serve the interests of the likes of the China Lobby.

The shift in the international opium traffic is also a metaphor for what has happened in Southeast Asia itself. As the U.S. has settled in there, its presence radiating a nimbus of genocide and corruption, armadas of airplanes have come to smash the land and lives of a helpless people; mercenary armies have been trained by the U.S.; and boundaries reflecting the U.S. desires have been established, along with houses of commerce and petty criminality created in the American image. One of the upshots has been that the opium trade has been systematized, given U.S. technological expertise and a shipping and transportation network as pervasive as the U.S. presence itself. The piratical Corsican transporters have been replaced by pragmatic technocrats carrying out their jobs with deadly accuracy. Unimpeded by boundaries, scruples, or customs agents, and nurtured by the free flow of military personnel through the capitals of the Orient, the United States has—as a reflex of its warfare in Indochina—built up a support system for the trade in narcotics that is unparalleled in modern history.

The U.S. went on a holy war to stamp out Communism and to protect its Asian markets, and it brought home heroin. It is a fitting trade-off, one that characterizes the moral quality of the U.S. involvement. This ugly war keeps coming home, each manifestation more terrifying than the last; home to the streets of the teeming urban ghettos and the lonely suburban isthmus where in the last year the number of teen-age heroin addicts has taken a quantum leap forward. Heroin has now become the newest affliction of affluent America—of mothers in Westport, Connecticut, who only wanted to die when they traced track marks on their daughters' elegant arms; or of fathers in Cicero, Illinois, speechless in outrage when their conscripted sons came back from the war bringing home a blood-stained needle as their only lasting souvenir.

2. Treasure Island: Bringing Home the Harvest

by Jon Stewart

Like an intercontinental ballistic boomerang, the war has come home.

Reliable accounts from officials in Vietnam set the current rate of heroin addiction in the American armed services at anywhere from 15 to 35 percent, or 20,000 to 70,000 monkeys groping for a fix. The figure for overall drug usage (including grass) is *conservatively* estimated at about 80 percent.

What that means when the statistics come off the printed page and take on flesh and blood is that something over 5,000 addicts will be settling in the San Francisco area alone during 1971. And that's to say nothing of the untold thousands who are returning home to Smalltown, America. Furthermore, since heroin only became significantly evident in Vietnam early in 1970, we are seeing only the first assault wave of strung-out vets. Lady Smack is known to be winning converts at an unprecedented rate, and it is not unrealistic to project a vision of half the American armed forces nodding out on sweet opiate dreams within another year.

Jon Stewart is associate editor of *Organ* magazine and a frequent contributor to *Ramparts*. Reprinted with permission from *Organ* (June 1971).

What that means in terms of the war effort is nothing compared to the specter of thousands of G.I.'s returning home with life-consuming habits. Young, middle-class Americans may learn very suddenly the meaning of the word "ghetto."

Until recently, the "drug problem" in Vietnam has been regarded by the press—and, consequently, the American people—as but another war-related atrocity that's happening "over there." Our consciences may be a little rattled over our morning coffee when we read an item on page 13, and maybe again during the evening news, just as it was a year ago when we began hearing reports of a certain massacre at My Lai. But such things have a way of fast turning into abstractions—distant, statistical, and faceless. We don't have to deal with them in our everyday lives. They're troublesome to think about, and too remote to comprehend.

Not so for the military addict. He may be troublesome, but he's neither remote nor faceless. His numbers are legion, and he's as close as the man walking beside you on the street. In fact . . .

Treasure Island Revisited

Treasure Island, contrary to popular opinion, is not located in some uncharted expanse of the Eastern Atlantic Ocean—a place known only to pirates like Long John Silver. The *real* Treasure Island is a low, man-made appendage to Yerba Buena Island,

and it lies in the middle of San Francisco Bay. In fact, it's only about three miles, via the Bay Bridge, from San Francisco. Furthermore, it is not inhabited by buccaneers (at least not the old-fashioned kind), but by about 10,000 Navy and civilian personnel. It's the Navy's largest "separation center," and serves as the site for several units of the Naval Schools Command. Most naval personnel returning from Asian duty pass through Treasure Island in the process of receiving discharge.

Among the thousands of returning veterans from Asia that come to Treasure Island every month, a sizable proportion are assigned to one of three barracks—204, 209.8 or 209.9. These are the outcastes—the dopers, murderers, rapists, thieves, homosexuals. They're on either legal hold or legal transit, and are awaiting courts-martial, summary hearings, and anything from a general to a dishonorable discharge.

Barracks 209.8, which we have had several occasions to visit over the past month, is known around the base as Doper's Barracks. *All* the men in 209.8, excepting the "pigs" and "spies," are dopers. At present there are about fifty men in the barracks. The turnover is high, and it is estimated that about 7,000 men a year pass through Barracks 209.8. Seven thousand dopers. The other two barracks are also "doper's barracks," though they have a share of other kinds of "criminals." 209.9 is a restricted barracks, and visitors are not welcome. The addicts there have a little trouble scoring their dope, but usually they just sneak over to 209.8, which adjoins it, and do up with the boys there. No *real* problem, just sort of an inconvenience. 204 is not restricted, but because it houses a number of homosexuals awaiting general discharges, the dopers there like to amble over to 209.8, where they're among their own kind. Birds of a feather fly together.

"THE NAVY IS LIKE A JOINT: THE MORE YOU SUCK, THE HIGHER YOU GET"—Graffito in 209.8.

On our first visit to Treasure Island we wandered among the monotonous two-story buildings looking for Barracks 209.8. Unable to locate it, even with the aid of a map, we finally approached a group of seamen and asked for directions. "You looking to score some dope?" they answered. "Hell, you don't have to go there to score. What do you want?"

Barracks 209 (divided into 209.8 and 209.9) is actually rather easy to find if you know what you're looking for. It's enclosed (unlike all the other barracks) behind a high wire fence, and a small guardhouse stands at the gate. Since it was empty, we passed through apparently unnoticed, quietly entered the front door (again unnoticed), passed by the office, and walked up to the second floor. We approached the first man we saw: "Hi, we hear this is the dopers' barracks."

"Sure," came the answer. "Have a toke."

For the rest of the day, and for several days following, we sat and talked with the men of 209.8, and with others from 204 who happened in. They were more than eager to talk to us, and insisted that they didn't give a damn about being identified or having their pictures taken. They were all due for discharge soon, and anyway, they despised the Navy and were glad someone was willing to listen.

The second floor of the barracks, now closed, was the scene of the hottest action, since it was farthest removed from the front office, where a martial-at-arms was always stationed. "Actually," said George Hayes, who had a bunk on the second floor, "the pigs leave us alone pretty much. They know what's happening, and they'd just rather not have to get involved. Some of them are just plain scared to come up here. They think we're all hardened criminals."

Hayes went on to tell about how they'd dealt with a master-at-arms, C. C. Gettys: "He'd been hassling us pretty heavy for a while, making busts, searching lockers, breaking up parties, so one afternoon we just dropped some very pure acid in his coffee. He really freaked. He went over to the first-aid station and told them he thought somebody's slipped him some acid, but since nobody knew for sure what was wrong with him, they couldn't give him no antidote. He couldn't even drive home. His old lady had to come pick him up and take him home. He's been O.K. since then, though."

Hayes and a group of friends were eager to show us their former "shooting gallery," the place where they used to retire to shoot skag (heroin). It was a room on the ground floor, between the two halves of Barracks 209. That week it had been closed and padlocked by MP's. Undaunted, someone found a crowbar, and within a few minutes the lock was off. The large room was completely empty, but the walls were covered with incredible wall paintings, drawings, and graffiti—psychedelic, sexual, and political. It might have been an empty meeting hall in the Haight-Ashbury. "We used to have lots of mattresses down here, and a good radio," George said. "We'd get about twenty guys down here, all doing acid or smack, and just lie back all night." Since the room had been padlocked, the large bathroom in the rear of the building had become the new shooting gallery.

Another popular location in 209.8 is Wolfman's Corner, a small area in a corner of the second floor, surrounded by high lockers. A table and several chairs suggest that the area might be a kind of small reading lounge, but the six-foot plastic marijuana plant that stands in the corner suggests otherwise. Indeed, Wolfman's Corner is another shooting gallery. Or was, until a recent tragedy made the place uncomfortable.

Life and Death in 209.8

On one of the lockers in Wolfman's Corner, a message is scrawled in pencil: *God, don't let me die here.* Underneath, it's signed: *Bijika.* The lettering is highly stylized, bold.

On August 28, 1970, Seaman "Chico" Bijika sat in Wolfman's Corner with four other seamen and stuck a needle in his arm. All five were hitting up their twice-daily dosage of smack, maintaining the habits they'd acquired in Vietnam. Seconds after Chico released the tourniquet from his arm, he closed his eyes and drooped his head. Richard Hadnett, one of the other four addicts, concerned about his buddy, reached for Bijika's spoon and was about to taste the cooked white powder when he noticed that Bijika's face was flushed. He put down the spoon and pulled open Bijika's eyes and listened to his heartbeat. His heart was pounding, and he was breathing. Hadnett and the others assumed that Bijika was just nodding out. But minutes later, the face across from them became very red; the eyes, pulled open once again, were white, except for bright red striations. Then they noticed his mouth was bleeding. His fingernails turned red and began to bleed. His ears began to bleed. And then his eyes bled, streaming red tears down his cheeks.

Hadnett and the others picked him up and started to walk him down the long hallway of the barracks toward the exit, since he still had some muscle tone. They figured to take him to first-aid and report that they'd found him OD'ed in the head. But halfway down the hall Chico convulsed. He fell into a fetal position on the floor and froze there like granite. "We couldn't even open his hands," reported one of the onlookers.

Chico never regained consciousness. Five days later, he died in the base hospital. Yes, Chico Bijika had OD'ed, all right; but not on heroin. He'd been sold a spoon of white powdered battery acid, scraped from a car battery. He burned to death, from inside out.

Bijika's story may be more sordid than most, but in other respects it is fairly typical of life in Barracks 209.8. He had been detained in "dopers' barracks" for eight months, awaiting discharge on grounds of a dope bust. The actual paperwork and official procedure leading to the discharge could have been accomplished in about two weeks, or a month at most. But Bijika was a heroin addict, and the Navy doesn't like addicts, so it kept him around and hassled him and busted him, and made life miserable for him. That's how the Navy deals with its addicts.

During Bijika's eighth month in 209.8, according to Richard Richards, a friend, he was summoned to the office of Naval Investigations and was offered an immediate discharge and the dropping of all charges against him if he'd finger two suspects in his own barracks. Bijika, sick of the Navy, sick of 209.8, sick of the continual hassles, agreed to rat on two seamen who were selling smack in the barracks. The Navy promised him he'd be discharged and on his way home before they would reveal their source of information. However, days before Bijika's discharge, information leaked through attorneys on the case that Bijika was the informant. The news spread throughout the barracks. That day, Bijika scored a hit from an unidentified barracks mate and shot his arm full of sulfuric acid. The murderers were never apprehended, though the men of Barracks 209.8 have little doubt about their identity. But of course they don't talk, and most of those who were there at the time are gone now anyway.

Wolfman's Corner was still being used when we first visited the barracks, but only by more recent "inmates."

The daily routine around 209.8 is the quintessence of monotony. Almost no one works, except for a few hours a day on guard duty inside the barracks or stationed outside in the guardhouse. The typical day in 209 begins with getting stoned, breakfast, getting stoned, lunch, getting stoned some more, dinner, followed by more dope, some acid maybe, then a brief period of unconsciousness after which it's time to do it up again before breakfast. The true junkies stay stoned pretty much all day and all night, and do nothing else but sleep, wash clothes, and drive into San Francisco to score more smack. The others, who aren't heavy into heroin—or at least aren't really hooked on it yet—spend most of the day passing hash pipes and talking about going home. Occasionally, the more active ones will go over to the gym and play basketball, or just turn on all the hot showers and take a "poor man's steam bath." It's deadly boring.

Since the returning dopers from Vietnam became almost too numerous to deal with at Treasure Island, the 12th Naval District, of which T.I. is the center, has instituted a program that is unique in the Navy. All men awaiting BCD (bad conduct discharge) or summary courts-martial are eligible to opt for an undesirable discharge and thus circumvent the long, drawn-out court-martial. The program has been so successful that it is now difficult to get on the roster of men willing to accept the UD. Though figures are not available to us as to the actual number of men who have accepted or are trying to get a UD, we were told that the list "is long and getting longer." Many of the men we interviewed said they would be happy to take a UD and get out, rather than wait around for the legal machinery to offer them a general discharge, which is not an honorable, but certainly preferable to the UD. They really don't care how the hell they get out; just so they get.

Busts are fairly frequent in 209.8. MP's will charge into the barracks for no apparent reason and check out footlockers, which almost always turn up something. The men are often searched for drugs while walking about the base, minding their own business. Military law is not subject to constitutional edicts regarding search and seizure.

Since the turnover of men in 209.8 is high, activities and moods vary considerably from week to week. We were told, for example, that had we come a month earlier we'd have found a barracks literally full of heroin addicts. As it was, only about 15 percent of the men were strung out behind horse. Possibly 50 percent of them used heroin, but only to supplement their regular diet of weed, hash, and acid. Even the "pigs" change from month to month, according to the men. Currently, one of the assistant masters-at-arms is himself a head, and regularly buys and sells dope in the barracks.

Typical Withdrawal Reactions: Inside Views

The following stories are taken directly from interviews with the men of 209.8. They vary little, even in details, and are representative of dozens of others' stories. When you get to know one Navy addict, you get to know hundreds, even thousands of Navy addicts.

Fisher

Danny Fisher, a twenty-one-year-old, had been back from Asia for only two weeks when we talked with him. He is soft-spoken, intense, intelligent, and politically radical. He was busted in Vietnam four months after he arrived there when he OD'ed on skag. He didn't have a habit at the time; in fact, he'd snorted heroin only a few times previously. The first time he shot up he OD'ed. He woke up in a military hospital and remembers seeing two doctors standing over him nodding their heads, saying, "Typical withdrawal reactions." He was arrested while still in the hospital, and soon transferred to the Long Binh Be Naval Hold, a sort of semirestricted area for detention of suspect or convicted Navy personnel. Most of the men at Long Binh were dopers. In fact, the unofficial sleeve patch worn by the men to identify their outfit was a circular patch with the words *Long Binh Be Legal Hold* stitched in psychedelic lettering around the perimeter, and a green marijuana plant in the center.

Fisher spent seven months at Long Binh, and it was while being held there that he developed his habit. "The mama-sans [Vietnamese women employed on bases as maids and scrubwomen] would bring it into the base and sell it, or you'd score from guys who had girls in town. It was never a problem getting it. Scag was just always there; everybody had it. Even in the brig you could get it." After Danny had had seven months of boredom, humiliation, and heroin addiction, the Navy decided to send him to Treasure Island for eventual discharge. He described his flight home to us: "When I left I had a habit of about two vials a day [about $12 in Vietnam]. I usually got off by snorting or shooting. Actually, the last time I got hooked I was mostly snorting, but before that I always shot it.

"The flight home was incredible. The flight from Tan Son Nhut airport in Saigon to Okinawa was about a three-and-a-half-hour flight. I experienced mainly chills and apprehension, knowing it was going to get worse. . . . I had a 'te-te' [a very small hit] just before leaving Saigon, but it wasn't enough to help much. We waited in Okinawa four hours and then had a seven-hour flight to Honolulu. There, I started getting pains in my joints, especially in my legs, and extreme chills and a headache. So we were there [Honolulu] a couple hours and then took off for about a four-hour flight to Travis [Air Force Base, east of San Francisco]. During that leg of it I got bad stomach convulsions, a pounding headache, and very dizzy. You get very nervous too, like hyperactive, full of nervous energy. I got up and walked to the front of the airplane, went to the bathroom, drank a cup of lemonade, went back to my seat, and sat down. Then, seconds later, I got up and went to the back of the airplane and did the same thing again. Then back to the front—just back and forth for like the whole goddamn trip. In Hawaii I damn near jumped the plane to get a fix. A lot of guys do that. Six of my friends on that plane were going through the same thing. I don't know how many more there might have been. I know some guys took stuff with them and smoked up on the trip and didn't have to come down until they got stateside. One guy I know went to Sacramento straight from Travis. He had three days before he had to report to T.I. He never has shown up."

Danny, like most of the G.I.'s who get strung out on heroin, had never used hard drugs before he went into the service. He'd done some grass and acid, but he'd stayed away from addictive drugs. "I had not only not done smack before going to Nam," he told us, "but I had never even considered the possibility of doing it. There it is, man. I was very down on hard drugs—like smack and coke—I wouldn't shoot speed with friends because I couldn't stand the idea of sticking a needle in my body."

Danny has pretty much kicked his habit, now, though he still scores a couple of dime bags a week. He has some trouble getting off behind the smack that's peddled stateside, though. It's only about 5 to 10 percent pure, compared to the 97 percent pure smack he was addicted to in Vietnam.

Kelly

Jim Kelly gave up his job selling vacuum cleaners in Colorado when he turned seventeen and joined the Navy. A year later he was an addict in Vietnam. He had a heavy habit, amounting to almost $20 a day in Nam. He turned himself in, was sent to Nhabe Legal Hold, and was held there for four months with other dopers. From Nhabe he was sent to Treasure Island for discharge, and confined in 209.8 again with the dopers. A friendly doctor on Treasure Island gave him a good supply of Thorazine to help him get through withdrawal, and told him not to tell anyone that he'd helped him out. After four months in 209.8, Kelly was back on smack regularly. While there he was busted three times, once for a one-day unauthorized absence, and twice for possession of narcotics. He spent twenty days in the brig, paid a $200 fine, was handed an undesirable discharge and escorted to the main gate. "And don't come back. You're not welcome here," they told him. Kelly is nineteen years old now. He hates the Navy. Would he still do heroin? "Sure, if you brought it around. I mean, I won't go out and look for it, but probably couldn't resist it if somebody lays it in front of me."

Rumplestiltskin

Rumplestiltskin (anonymous) is waiting for a general discharge, doing his time in 209.8. He was an "Air Force brat" before entering the Navy, and held very conservative political attitudes. He had never done any dope at all. While attending school for electronics at Treasure Island in 1968 he got turned on to grass. "There weren't many dopers around then," he told us. "And if anybody got busted they got Red Line Brig and hard labor. Then a dishonorable." He shipped overseas on the carrier *Constellation* late in 1968 and didn't notice much dope, aside from grass and hash, at that time. But a year later, on a second tour, "Man, the shit was all over the place. I was on coke then, and used to have to have it sent to me by mail aboard the ship. So, I started mixing my coke with smack, and before I knew it I had a Jones [a habit]. I just tried to stay as muddleheaded as possible. I hated the fucking Navy, and so did the other dopers. We used to sabotage the fucking ship. We'd short out all the sound-powered phones on board. Once, when the President came aboard with all his emergency communications equipment, we cut the hot line."

Back in the states, he went AWOL and wasn't discovered until two months later when he was busted in San Francisco for possession of grass and a rig.

He spent seventeen days in city jail before the Navy bothered to come and get him, then was fined $200 and received a four-month suspended sentence by the Navy on Treasure Island.

He recalls when he first got to Treasure Island: "We used to have basketball games. The Psychedelics against the Downers. And whenever we were given a job to do, like clean up around the barracks, we'd just find a speed freak and turn him on and let him do it. The speed freaks would be running around working their asses off, and the rest of us would do smack, or whatever we were into, and lie back and watch." Tom Sawyer revisited.

Mike Stryjewski, AMS 3, petty officer, went to Vietnam a year and a half ago. At that time he had never used a hard drug, and weighed in at a healthy 165 pounds. When he returned one year later he had a heroin habit that cost him $40 a week in Vietnam (equivalent to about $400 a week in San Francisco), and he weighed 125 pounds.

Mike, a handsome, intelligent, soft-spoken man of twenty-one, told us about his first contact with skag: "I was in Nam about a week and a half before I came across any. We went to this whorehouse and we were just sitting around smoking jays of Cambodian red, and these brothers came in and sat down and passed some skag around—snorting it, you know. A guy could spill a dime [$10 worth of heroin] on the floor and it wouldn't even matter; they'd just form another hit. So they passed it to me and I tried it. And it was good, you know. I got sick first, but then it was really good."

Mike didn't start shooting smack until he was returned to the States. "The stuff you get here," he said, "is so weak that you have to shoot it to get off. And besides, it's too expensive here to smoke—it all goes up in smoke. But over there, it's so pure, man, you don't even have to burn it. You just mix it with a little water, just like that."

Before getting busted for possession in Vietnam, Mike was a helicopter crewman. He testified that most of the crewmen aboard helicopters are either heavily into dope—mostly smack—or alcohol. "There's just no other way, man," he says. "When I'd get my orders for the next day and I'd know I had to go out, I was fucking scared. So we'd just load up on smack. We'd make up a whole pack of jays, and take it with us and just stay stoned all day. We'd just sit back and enjoy the ride and hope nothing would happen."

Mike figures that about 80 percent of the men stationed in his area were freaks of one kind or another. In his barracks of ninety men, excepting the lifers and officers, there were thirty enlisted men who were definitely strung out on smack. Most of the others were on grass or alcohol. Mike was able to support his habit off his paycheck and a little black-market dealing, "but the guys with really bad habits had to buy and sell to make it."

Asked about dealing and corruption among the Vietnamese officialdom, Mike confessed to never having come into direct contact with it. "But you know damn well they're into it. They have to be. It's so wide open. The 'white mice' [Nationalist police] and QC [military police] are outrageous. You have to pay them off for everything. It's like in Tijuana, only multiplied tenfold. They bust you and just automatically expect to be bought off. They'll come up to you and before they even bust you they'll start dealing with you for a payoff. At LBJ [Long Binh Jail], which is like a big brig for all the branches of the service, the security is like really tight, but there's no problem about scoring dope. The guards'll sell it to you."

George Hayes, who "used to be a gung-ho pig with the Armed Forces Police," confirmed Mike's allegations about corruption among the police: "We'd go into some village on a panty raid, you know, and we'd always find a couple dudes who'd been over the hill for a couple months. We'd take them and turn them over to CID. But first we'd rip off their stash. One day we busted this dude who was tripping around the village, playing it cool, dodging in and out of this place and that, collecting taxes, you know. He was a gook. So we popped him, right. And this dude had a briefcase full of smack, man. I tried to talk the lifer I was with into ripping it off, you see, and shooting the gook, and taking the money. The lifer wouldn't do it, man. But this gook had such a stash on him—like $25,000 worth of smack on him, plus all this change. If we hadn't been in the middle of the fucking street, I'd a shot the fucking lifer *and* the gook and taken the stash. I was a hard-assed dude, then. I really would of."

Mike seriously considered staying in Vietnam where he could easily support his habit, rather than face coming home. He claims that large numbers of AWOL G.I.'s have done just that. Vietnamese women, particularly the prostitutes, think it's a symbol of status to have a G.I. shacked up with them, he claims. "The women don't seem to like their own men. They'll give you a place to stay, buy your dope for you—really take care of you." Others opt for the six-month extension of duty with a two-week vacation anyplace they want to go. Bangkok is a favorite rest-and-recuperation station because the dope there is even better and cheaper than in Nam. "A lot of guys that were shooting up," said Mike, "didn't even think twice about coming home."

Despite the urge to stay, Mike accepted his orders for transfer to Treasure Island, where he would be placed on legal hold, pending investigation. Before he passed through customs in Saigon, en route home, he scored a hit of smack from a cab driver at the airport to help him through the long flight. He was afraid to try to bring anything aboard the plane, though as it turned out he was never searched. "That lasted me until I got to Okinawa, then I started going through withdrawals in the plane. I almost jumped the plane in Hawaii, but a buddy talked me out of it. By the time I got to Travis I was a mess—shivering and puking my guts out. I had a three-day leave, so I went and stayed with my brother-in-law in San Jose. I couldn't sleep the whole three days. When I got to T.I. they assigned me to 204, and the first thing I did was go over to 209 and score a hit." Mike is still doing smack, though not regularly. His discharge has finally come through, and he plans to go home to Montana.

All the men of 209.8 want to go home. The exclusive topics of conversation in the barracks are of scoring dope and going home. Of course, the two ideas may be mutually exclusive. Most of the men are from small towns in the Midwest and western states like Montana, Colorado, New Mexico, and Oregon. They'll find it harder to score their brand of dope back there than it is on Treasure Island, where there's a steady influx from San Francisco and Travis and the ships returning from Asia. They'll have to settle for one or the other—hometown or dope—and the cards are stacked against them, to say the least. Still, everyone believes he can make the transition.

So the days come and go at 209.8, but without much definition. No one knows for sure just when he'll get out. Everyone expects to be hassled, detained, lied to, busted, confined to brig, bribed, humiliated. The easiest way to deal with it is to stay stoned, twenty-four hours a day. And so they do—on grass, hash, speed, acid, coke, smack. They make the time pass as obliviously as possible.

It's difficult to guess what will happen to them. Some may indeed kick junk and stay clean in their midwestern hometowns, smoking a little grass on weekends and drinking lots of beer during the week. Others will certainly return to the city, probably San Francisco, and submit to life-consuming addictions.

Whatever becomes of them, the soldier-addicts represent a new breed in America: a new breed of Navy, a new breed of veteran, a new breed of junkie.

Postscript

On our last visit to Treasure Island Naval Station, made for the purpose of confirming information and getting a few more photographs, Bob (the photographer) and I got a taste of the kind of treatment the men of 209.8 are continually subjected to.

While sitting on bunks inside 209.8, talking with two seamen, we were approached by the barrack's chief and told to go to the front office. There we were held until the chief of naval investigations, the base chief, about six MP's and investigators, and security agents arrived. The two seamen were taken into the main part of the barracks by most of the mob, and Bob and I were left under the guard of the master-at-arms, a genial enough young man who was obviously scared shitless. There was trouble in his barracks. He asked that if we were holding dope we get rid of it through the open window before the investigators came back in. We didn't have anything, nor had we had anything, nor had the seamen been holding.

Shortly, the mob came into the office, read us our rights, placed us under arrest for "suspicion of dealing with dangerous drugs and narcotics on a United States military base," and handcuffed us. We were searched thoroughly, marched out the door with the two seamen past cheering crowds of dopers who'd gathered to witness the latest bust, put in a truck, and hauled off to the Investigations Office.

We were held for two hours before being allowed to make phone calls. In the meantime, we were questioned in tiny, separate interrogation rooms, fingerprinted, and mug-shot for permanent government police files. After five hours of stifling heat and claustrophobia we were brought into the office of Thomas Prettyman chief of naval investigation, and told that the dope charge had been dropped, and we were being charged with violation of trespass rules, a charge which was obviously trumped up as an excuse for kicking us off the base. We were both issued *persona non grata* walking papers, and told that if we ever appeared on the base again we would be subject to arrest and six months in jail and a $500 fine. Bob was given a military escort off base, and I was turned over to the San Francisco police, who had traffic warrants out for my arrest. I paid my traffic fines and walked out of the Hall of Justice a free man, finally.

Being civilians, we were treated with some caution by the military, through Prettyman (a civilian employee) was generally rude. He naturally associated us with the men of 209.8, whom he obviously loathes.

When we left, the two seamen who were arrested with us were still in handcuffs and were being led from the investigation office by MP's. We called after them, and asked that they call us as soon as they were released. Two weeks later, we received a call from Treasure Island. The men had just been released. They had spent fourteen days in the brig, during which time no formal charges had ever been brought against them, and no lawyer had visited them, though they had repeatedly asked to see one.

But of course, they're used to it. It was just the normal kind of hassle around 209.8. They've learned that it's to be expected, and they've learned how to cope with it—they stay stoned.

3. The U.S. Army: Amnesty Unlimited

by David Raskin

The following is a transcription of a tape recording made by Lieutenant David Raskin in June 1971. Lieutenant Raskin was at that time serving as director of an Army "amnesty program" drug treatment center near the Mekong Delta region of Vietnam. Though more complete information available to the editors of Organ *shows that the National Liberation Front of South Vietnam is in no way involved in drug traffic, the interview nonetheless offers special insight into one of the Army's principal amnesty centers.*

My new thing is junkies. Let me explain my job. The Army, of course, is a pig outfit with a police mentality. To their minds possession of drugs is a legal problem, but the overwhelming number of strung-out G.I.'s have begun to make them realize that something has to be done, so they've begun what they call an "amnesty program." "Amnesty" means that if you are using drugs you can go to your commanding officer and say, "I am using heroin," which constitutes an admission of guilt. And his

David Raskin has recently returned from military duty in Vietnam, where he was responsible for a drug amnesty program. Reprinted with permission from *Organ* (June 1971).

commander will say, "That's great, I grant you amnesty. I will not bust you for admitting to me you use heroin. However, tomorrow if we find you with heroin we'll put you in jail."

The people down at the grass roots realize this is just a sham, a joke, unless you can offer the guy some way to stop using the drug. So we've been opening up centers where what they actually do is go cold turkey. We give them some tranquilizers and medicine for cramps, shit like that, and try and help them out, help them through their withdrawal, and we have group therapy sessions and individual therapy sessions. You know, try and work it out so the the cat won't go back on skag [heroin].

Nobody knows how to cure junkies, nobody knows how to cure alcoholics, so nobody's got any hard figures on success rates, but probably the average halfway house in Vietnam is about 10 to 20 percent, which is much higher than the ones in the States.

The reason for that is the guys who use heroin here smoke it and their habits aren't as bad as the people back in the United States, 'cause they aren't shooting it and a lot of people back in the United States have been using it for years and years and years. The average guy over here has been using it for just a few months. So it all adds up to not as bad a habit and therefore an easier time getting off and staying off.

Anyway, the heroin over here runs about twenty times the concentration and about one-twentieth the price of heroin in "the world." Heroin in "the world" is about 5 to 10 percent pure, and here it's 90 to 100 percent pure. A five-dollar cap of heroin here would cost about $100 in the States, comparable purity and all, so that a guy who's on a ten-dollar habit here would be on a two-hundred-dollar habit in the States. And to let you know how big it is, some guys here are on fifty-dollar-a-day habits, so when you multiply that by twenty you begin to understand the quantity of pure heroin that's being smoked around this place.

Most junkies in the States don't want to quit; they love the drug too much, and the problems that they have in their lives are too overbearing; they can't deal with them and the heroin is a lot nicer to them than reality. But this is a different population over here, this is the All-American Boy. This is not the middle-city, ghetto person, not the hard-core poverty type who's suffering from racism and a fucked-up economic system and living with rats and all this kind of shit. This is the boy next door, the blond-haired, blue-eyed boy next door. He's not even the draftee. A lot of these guys are enlisted, go in the Army, rah, rah, the whole thing. Some of them even think of the Army in terms of a career. It's not the typical image of the junkie.

A lot of studies have been done on the amount of addiction, but they haven't been published or publicized—they've been done by independent dudes like myself who have just been working with the problem and decided to get down and do a study. The averages show that between 10 and 40 percent of any given unit is strung out on smack. I would say a realistic average for all enlisted men, rank E-5 and below [E-5 is buck sergeant—three stripes], is approximately 20 to 25 percent using heroin. Now that's horrendous; that is phenomenal in itself. I don't think that's an exaggeration at all. Even if it were just 10 percent—now that's the minimum estimate based on highly scientific studies—that's a lot of junkies. And that's not a static number because they're always going home and there are new ones coming in and getting strung out all the time.

Last year, if you remember all the guys coming back from Vietnam, all the talk was about the dynamite grass—Thai flower grass and Cambodian red and Mekong Delta green and all this real dynamite grass. All that's true; the local grass is about the heaviest in the world. But there was no heroin. All of a sudden last year, during the summer, large quantities of heroin started appearing out of nowhere, literally out of nowhere. Like magic, overnight heroin was everywhere. It wasn't a chance happening, it wasn't something that happened like a natural process of any kind. It was well planned—logistics and everything. I'm sure of it. It's not the military paranoid mind hard at work—it's just so obvious that when there's no heroin in Vietnam for years and years and years and all of a sudden, in a month's time, it's everywhere, that somebody made plans to deliver it in large quantities and at cheap prices.

Other things have happened since that time . . .

they noticed that in a week's time this one type of vial [the heroin comes in little plastic vials—some of them have brand names on them] showed up everywhere from the Delta to the DMZ in a week's time. Some large supplier had turned loose this new type of vial filled with heroin in a matter of a week all across the country. We know it's not a small operation. It's not a bunch of independent small-time dealers just smuggling it a kilo at a time across the Cambodian border, although I am sure that after the initial big boys moved in there's a lot of small-time operators doing a lot of business. But essentially it's a large operation.

Now the two major theories that exist over here are the Communist Plot Theory, which at any other time of my life would have seemed ludicrous beyond words but now seems completely plausible . . . and that's that the Communists are unable to defeat us militarily so they've turned to psychological warfare and propaganda, like the United States. It's become a public relations war being fought in the newspapers. Nixon with his POW's and Hanoi saying "Right on" to the peace marchers.

People believe that the Communists are disseminating the heroin to destroy American troops, not with bullets but with drugs, and at some given point the supply will be cut off and large numbers of American G.I.'s will be incapacitated and unable to fight or do anything and the Communists will have a chance to move in and do some heavy-duty killing. Either that, or on a large scale sending thousands and thousands of junkies to the United States and further adding to the decay of the fiber of our society.

So these are two ideas of why the Communists would want to push drugs in on the Americans. They've found VC carrying kilos of heroin and they know that the Laotians are heavy into manufacturing heroin. Possession of opium is legal in Laos if you have a license, and the name of the game up there is corruption. All you have to do to get a license is have enough money, and then you can carry heroin, make heroin, grow opium, do anything you want. It's that simple. As a matter of fact the U.S. just launched a protest with the Laotian government because this Air America, which is a "private company," but *actually* CIA-operated, is a major means of transportation around Southeast Asia. Everybody flies Air America, and these Laotian dudes were using Air America to transport their heroin, so there was some bitching and moaning about that. Anyway, there is good evidence that the Communists are shipping it into the country. It comes in several ways, out of Hong Kong on airplanes, smuggled in by airline stewardesses, Vietnamese government officials, civilians, etc. It comes down the Mekong River out of Laos and Cambodia into the Mekong Delta and it's brought in by VC.

The second paranoid theory about where the drugs come from is the International Crime Theory. The Mafia and "them" boys, trying to drum up a lot of business for when the boys come marching home. You know, when Johnny comes marching home we'll have his twenty-five-cent bag and his fix waiting for him, we'll sell him a set of works, and business will keep booming. There is evidence for this theory too. Some G.I.'s who have come back from Vietnam have reported to their local authorities that people have approached them upon their arrival at home. You know, a guy does his year in Vietnam, goes home to wherever, he's home for two days, and some dude comes knocking on the door, says, "Hi, my name's George. I understand you just got back from Vietnam and you were strung out on skag, and we could work out a deal for regular supply." This kind of thing. The talk that goes on about this is endless. Nobody really knows, but those are the two major theories with evidence behind them and they are probably *both* true.

Heroin is a very seductive drug. To make an analogy—it's like women. In your barely post-pubic years when you've never tasted of the woman's flesh, you really don't get horny, you don't really long for women beside you because you really don't know what it is. You have these faint feelings in your crotch, but when you've made love to a woman then you know there is nothing like it in the whole world. It's that simple. And you've always got to have more. You'll be horny for the rest of your life. And it's the same thing with heroin. It's a very seductive drug. Once you've tasted it it's very hard to stay away from it, even though you know that if you continue to use it you'll probably have a five-year life expectancy or you'll OD or you'll get some of it in your lungs by sniffing it or snorting it or smoking it and you'll get this chemical phenomena that will kill you in a few days and there's no treatment for it, and that you'll lose forty, fifty, sixty pounds and become a walking skeleton and you'll have to dedicate the rest of your life to hustling for smack. You know all those things in your mind, but you can't help yourself. And that's what these guys are up against.

Guys think that if they smoke heroin they won't get busted because the officers can't smell it. A cat'll stand out there in front of his captain smoking heroin right in his face and the guy'll never know it 'cause it has no odor, especially if it's mixed with tobacco. It just smells like a cigarette and so it's the easiest thing in the world. It's as easy to get as air, really.

Back to my job. I'm director of a program here near the hospital. I started out being a part-time helper. Our doctor, the psychiatrist, got transferred up north to some kind of road-building unit to be their battalion surgeon, and I got stuck with running the whole fucking show. So I'm in charge of one hundred Vietnamese amputees and who knows how many American junkies. It's really heavy, man, let me tell you. These dudes run down some heavy raps about how fucked up their heads are, how fucked up their lives are in Vietnam and why they started on heroin, and they all say they're going to stay off it, and then when they leave the program a week later most of them are back smoking skag. So I don't know where it's all going to end. I really don't, it's such a heavy problem. I think the only way to end it is to get everybody back where they belong, where they should have been all the time, back home. But anyway, there it is. I don't know what else to say about it. A quarter of the people in Vietnam are junkies. Think about that. Super heavy.

4. Turkey: Our War against the Peasants

by Jemima Kallas

In summertime, as long as one can remember, there have been fields of waist-high, lilac-white flowers bending gently with the breeze on the plains and mountains of Anatolia in Turkey. The opium poppy, mainstay of the Turkish economy and prime source of painkilling morphine used in hospitals throughout the world, will soon be a forbidden crop, alive only in the reminiscent tales of old men in the coffeehouses.

From the summer of 1972, "opium" will have dropped out of the living language in Turkey to become instead a memory, a ghost of a sometime prosperity, done in by the vagaries of international diplomacy and the skyrocketing rate of heroin addiction in a distant American culture. The name of the richest of the Turkish provinces, Afyon, given for the opium which grows there, will become a philologist's curiosity, a relic of a crop and an agricultural disaster which time will bury in the history books of Turkey. To the Turkish peasant, who has no use for the hallucinogenic effects of drugs derived from the poppy, but who depends on it only as a cash crop, it is hardly clear why he should be penalized for what

Jemima Kallas is an internationally known Turkish journalist and author. This article was specially prepared for *Smack!*

Americans at home or in Vietnam choose to shoot into their veins. Turks, although they live right in the middle of the stuff, have never been addicts. But to the new prime minister, Nihat Erim, who can ill afford the displeasure of his powerful, aid-granting NATO ally, it has been made all too clear that regardless of what internal problems he may face, the only course for Turkey is the eradication of opium as a Turkish crop.

Turkey's decision to wipe out a crop which brings in $3–4 million a year in official exports came neither suddenly nor easily. The story began in 1958, when Americans first awoke to the danger of drugs in their society. At that time, there was opium growing in 42 of Turkey's 67 provinces, maturing to a rich crop with a 12 to 15 percent morphine content, the highest raw morphine yield in the world. The harvest was under government control, but no licensing system ensured that what was sown and what was handed over to the man from the government tallied.

In 1958, the year that the Turkish lira was devalued 300 percent by the uneasy government of Adnan Menderes, U.S. Secretary of State Christian Herter let it be known that too much Turkish opium was going astray and it was time the country curbed production. With other worries on his hands, Menderes procrastinated. The 1960 army coup hung him before he acted, but in 1961 the generals themselves, just before handing over power to the people, cut the number of officially producing provinces to 21.

From 21, the number dropped in dribs and drabs until it reached 7 in 1970, but it dropped against a background of furious Turkish resentment and authoritarian U.S. pressure. "We are not responsible for the degeneracy of American youth," stormed former Prime Minister Suat Hayri Urguplu. Last year, President Nixon had this on his desk from a backwoods Turkish villager: "Who is America? I challenge her to fight. Tell her to come out and face me."

Each move to ban production in another province was squeezed out of a reluctant Turkish government. In area after area, the farmers had one year in which to think of something else to sow, or draw in their belts. In a country where literacy is still at a premium and farming is done with oxen and wooden hay forks, just what to plant instead of a traditional crop is something a peasant is more likely to look to Allah for than find out for himself. Protests and demonstrations flared up, but they were nothing the military police couldn't cope with.

The last provinces to survive in production were saved not by a procession of pitchforks against the local country hall, but by votes. Former Prime Minister Süleyman Demirel, who was peremptorily unseated on March 12, 1971, by a "new broom" government under army auspices, banked on the votes of his own province, the opium-growing area of

Isparta, to keep him in office. Isparta, as a result, was spared until the 1972 harvest, along with Kütahya, the constituency of the former Minister of Finance Mesut Erez, the vast opium granary of Afyon, and the fields of Burdur, where the milk is richest of all.

The U.S. Congress and the Senate, with the figure of heroin addicts in America skyrocketing every year, had no sympathy for Demirel's problems at home or the plight of the Turkish peasant. Several motions were put through to cut off all aid to any country continuing to produce opium. When the army brought in Professor Nihat Erim as prime minister, the message was clear. After three months of talks in Washington and Ankara, during which Erim wrung out what concessions he could, the foregone conclusion was made official: Turkey will no longer grow opium for the world.

To suffer the loss of so valuable a crop because of the caprice of another culture, especially one so affluent in comparison to his own, is hard medicine for the Turkish peasant to swallow. Turks aren't, and never have been, addicts. The peasants see opium as just another crop, a tough one with several agricultural advantages and the highest selling price on both its milk and its oil grain.

The hallucinogenic properties of what they have out in the fields is known to the farmers, but local taboos keep them disinterested. The biggest taboo is that it saps potency. Turks place high store on potency, as any people would where the winter nights are long and there is no electricity. They are also very concerned about their children, and another belief held is that taking opium makes for a malformed child.

Opium has altogether a sinister ring about it within the villages. If an adolescent happens to experiment and something happens to him afterward, they see an immediate cause and effect. A teacher in Kütahya had been bucked in the face by his horse when, as a boy, after playing around with opium, he mistook the horse for a cat and pulled its tail. He got no sympathy from his neighbors.

"My father used to force my mother to add opium to the baby's feed when it was crying all night. She didn't want to, but what could she do? My brother's grown up an idiot," said one farmer in a Circassion opium village in Burdur.

No, opium the drug is definitely not for humans in Turkey. They used to feed it to the water buffaloes in the winter to make them fight, and they still use it as a backrub, in cough medicines, but its value to the Turkish peasant is as a crop, not an escape.

Even without the black market, growing opium is one of the most profitable choices a Turkish farmer has. His legal yield from the plant far outweighs any other crop. This is partly because the poppy is so versatile. From the milk, he gets a government price of $9 to $12 per kilo, and farmers average a yearly 1 to 2 kilos per decare (1 acre = 0.247 decare). Then, from the grain, he averages $30 per decare to the local grain pressers, who turn it into the oil that runs the farmer's kitchen. The nearly drained-out pods are sold off to Holland for another $2 per decare production, the stalks serve for fuel, the waste product of the grain is turned into animal fodder, and the fresh leaves, before they become tough and poisonous, are used as spring salads. No wonder, then, that the farmer is angry when the American government, because it cannot or will not control those powerful interests profiting from the illegal drug trade, instead aims its full force at him, saying, "Change your way of life. Find some other way to make a living. What you're doing is bothering us."

But international politics and aid being what they are, it is the farmer who must change. It will not be an easy change, for opium is a traditional crop, and the rhythm of the countryside moves gracefully around it. Much that is new will have to replace the old.

The first sowing sequence begins in October and November. Any kind of ground can be used. You used to be able to see the bulbous green heads of the pods by the road through Corum to the old Hittite capital. Also, we knew they grew, hidden from government eyes, on the stony slopes of mountain plantations.

At planting time, the men leave the cafés and the long afternoon of tea in the autumn, and go out into the fields to sow. The seed is saved from the oil factories and scattered by hand from a bag carried under the arm. After that, there is nothing more to do, except watch. Winters can ruin the crop. They are bitter in Anatolia, and though snow does no harm to the seeded fields, covering them like a warm blanket, early frost locks the earth hard and smothers the life out of the seeds. Frost is the only and the ultimate hazard to the poppy farmer while the plant is growing, for the poppy is immune to all normal pests. Some farmers prefer to guard themselves against frost by making only a spring planting, but such plants are never as strong.

By March, the Koran readings that filled the winter evenings while the girls sewed their trousseaus are over. In the opium fields, the jagged leaves of the winter sowing push up. The women go out into the fields and hoe the ground to let in the air and clear away the weeds. They work in groups of four to six, doubled up like clothespins. From afar, they seem like bright flowers in the field, an array of spotted blues, greens, and reds, wearing the all-purpose Turkish trousers or several layers of petticoats that are mended in a patchwork of clashing colors and patterns.

By late March, the raggedly sown powdery greens of the poppy are thickening amid the fresh green of the wind-blown seeded lettuces. The women hoe again. In May, the buds form and the long stalks begin to grow. The stalk will grow under the blossom for about 3 to 6 feet, until the ground level is camouflaged by field after field of white and purple flowers. The flowers bloom for two weeks, and then fade and drop, leaving free the green head that carries next year's grains, and the precious ripening harvest of opium milk.

Two or three weeks after the petals fall, sometime in June, the farmers harvest. Everyone, from the smallest child tall enough to reach, goes into the fields to slit the buds with a scimitar-shaped pocketknife, so that the milk will trickle out. Some regions cut a three-quarter circle around the fat of the bud, others make a series of vertical slashes, and others prick the pod with holes until the milk beads out like a pincushion.

The milk oozes forth in a slow liquid stream that needs 24 hours to harden before it can be harvested. Those times are more crucial even than the winter frosts. One shower of rain can wash away the year's income. There is no government subsidy to support the crop, so should it rain, the farmer can only depend on the milk of the later-ripening spring sowing. Fortunately, the Anatolian climate is no given to rain in the summer. All being well, the villagers return to the fields a day later to pick off the spot of toffee-textured milk clinging to each pod. It is wrapped in vine leaves to keep it clean and stored away in sacks. When the harvest is completed, the farmer has only to bring his sacks of raw opium to the government officials at the Soil Products Office in the nearby town. There he may hand over the acrid-smelling crop and pocket the price. Recently, even this step has been simplified. With funds from a U.S. loan intended to advise villagers on alternate crops, the government bought cars so that official collectors could drive out to the villages (wherever roads exist) and collect the harvest on the spot. Thus logically the government should control the harvest.

The Anatolian villager is a poor man. It's a simple arithmetic that tells him that while an opium harvest gives the best price for what his land produces, black-market opium gives an even better one. Often the local landlord has the farmer deeply in debt. Many of the young men are forced to go off to do construction work in the towns in the summers so as to pay off debts that inflation has forced on them and their families. Others simply leave to work in German factories or emigrate to Australia. Thus the choice between a government price of $9 to $12 and a black-market $25, or even $50 if the quality is superb, is too clear to need much thought. In villages where the head gives the lead, there is smuggling; in others, probably not: the black-market areas are scattered throughout the countryside.

The smuggling operation usually starts sometime in the early summer when an agent comes out to the countryside to assess the quality of the crop and look around for sellers. At that time, if the farmers are desperate for money, the agent will pay for the opium in advance, but at a cut-rate price. Otherwise money changes hands after the harvest.

Late July and August, under cover of darkness, trucks draw up at the nearest road junction and wait for the villagers carrying the raw opium in sacks on their donkeys. Because it is the Turkish tradition, most villagers are armed, and the smugglers are armed superlatively. If a local gendarmerie unit attempts an ambush with the official blunderbusses, the chances are they will be beaten off, so there is seldom any problem. Once the opium is aboard, the responsibility for transport is with the truck driver, who must somehow get his sacks of strong-smelling illegal produce to one of the porters or to the go-between at the Syrian frontier. This problem is eased a bit because Turkey is so bitterly poor. The government officials, on the $60 to $75 a month, can often be bribed to turn a blind eye to what is going on.

To kill smuggling, a measure was passed after the 1960 revolution requiring all fields to be registered. The opium farmer was to inform the Soil Products Office of the area he intended to sow and the crop he expected. Checks were to be made by the Office to see to it he was telling the truth.

The system worked tolerably well until in 1971 a formal licensing system was introduced. But opium is a notoriously capricious crop. The farmers can't predict the exact yield. Nonetheless, they are fined if the harvest drops below the estimate. Therefore, the estimate is always cautious, and the overflow finds other outlets. In addition, until the 1968 loan for policing equipment introduced one or two helicopters, fields off the road were virtually impossible to discover or control.

As it is, until this spring, the American side estimated up to 80 percent of illegal heroin entering the U.S. to be of Turkish origin. The Turks have countered with growing figures of police hauls of smuggled opium and morphine base. The U.S. Bureau of Narcotics and Dangerous Drugs (BNDD) statistic of 80 percent has in fact been shaded to 60 to 80 percent in recent press releases. Sixty or 80, Turkey doesn't do too well on the illegal dollars. Far from being an unorthodox dollar income, the money is filtered into the smuggling chain in a way to drain the country even further. Opium gains are exchanged outside the country by the Istanbul speculators for Czech guns, American cigarettes, and French cosmetics. The smuggled goods are then flooded onto the impoverished domestic market. The farmer is richer, but the economy never sees an extra dime.

What other crops are there? After all, the 75,000 families that the final move to ban production outright will dispossess are not the first to feel the weight of misfortune. There are thousands of other peasant families who never had the benefit of opium's rich yield. Sugar beet is the highest money producer: a one-decare field gives one to two tons at $60 to $80 minus $15 expenses. However, the government allowed itself to be oversupplied with sugar beets in the fifties, and there is no room for further production.

Alfalfa, the animal fodder, gives 40 kilos of seeds every two years, netting $80, or $40 a year. An annual method of harvesting increases the income to $60, but as animal husbandry is not an important factor in the opium-growing districts, potential stocks of alfalfa have little outlet under present marketing conditions.

Growers of Turkish tobacco face the common price support paradox. Some of the best tobacco of the world comes from Turkey, and a decare field gives 100 kilos of leaves, at $130, minus $20 expenses. The drawback is that the international market is limited, and Turkish tobacco farmers find themselves throwing away their crops so as to keep up prices artificially, which effectively cuts their annual income. Sunflower nets $35, wheat and straw $35. Market gardening is not feasible on an economic scale under the present transport and irrigation system, particularly in the traditional poppy grounds on the slopes.

The prices of most crops except opium were raised 66 percent after 1970 devaluation in a tactful scheme by former Prime Minister Süleyman Demirel to edge farmers away from opium toward crops that were becoming progressively more attractive to grow. Opium still won out, but had Demirel stayed, he might have tightened the financial screws further and brought about "voluntary" change.

Most farmers emerging from a winter income have to borrow to tide them over to the harvest sales. The longer the loan, the higher the interest. The poppy is the farmer's bankroll: it redeems his loans, pays his bride price, and insures him against acts of God. The winter crop of opium is harvested as early as late June, so he can shorten the length of his loan.

If frost ruins the winter crop, he can sow again in spring. If the spring crop fails too, he still has the time to sow once more, and plant barley. No other crop is so flexible. It even enriches the soil, unlike most other crops, which drain it. Finally, local customs have clustered around the poppy during the centuries it has been cultivated. In some areas, for instance, the farmers save up for the bride price of the newborn son's future wife by burying a little of their opium harvest every year. The raw opium stays fresh underground, and by the time the baby is a man, the hidden cache can ultimately finance an honorable price even in these days of inflation.

Moving to the new is not simple. There were plans in 1968 to use half of a $3 million U.S. loan on educating the farmer to use his land more productively. There is no question that education could help, what with wheat fields that look like stubble before harvest and that grow so sparsely one could ride a bicycle between the clumps. However, neither the Turkish nor the U.S. government has got around to implementing this with experts or cash, and the improvement money is now being channeled into the hands of those controlling the other half of the loan, which has been used, most effectively, for policing.

It was one of the rumored conditions of Nihat Erim's surrender this July that Turkey should not only receive financial compensation, based on the sum the country stands to lose if crops for the next five or ten years sell at 1971 yields and prices, but that it should receive substantial manpower aid to help the villagers set up export-oriented productive schemes, from carpet weaving to small canning units. One feels, however, that if the money already appropriated was not used to help the farmer in three years, it is not likely that new schemes are going to appear to help him replace his lost earnings in the twelve months that are left between now and the last legal harvest he may make in 1972.

However, money is always cheaper to hand over than intelligence. As it happens that Turkey has had a record harvest this year, it is likely the compensation will be high. The government has made an all-out effort to induce the peasants not to go onto the black market, so as to boost officially received production figures. The radio put out appeals for 20 days running that seem to have struck home: in 1971 the Soil Products Office will receive 150 tons of opium, compared to 66 tons in 1970 from the same four provinces. That's not to say the peasants are happy with the change. The only reason there are no public protests this year is because of martial law and a certain amount of prudent censorship. An American television team touring the poppy fields with a police guard was swept straight past the site of a minor demonstration and only informed 24 hours later, mostly as a matter of academic interest, of what they had missed.

Turkey has now been forced by international politics into making a clean break. The crop that is too hot to handle stops, and Turkey is left, if it chooses to do so, with the business of rehabilitating its farmers. The farmers all have one or two other crops which will keep them from stark ruin. Since the tendency is already for village life to splinter and scatter into the towns, a move that the disaster in the opium fields will accelerate rather than introduce, perhaps the end of opium as a crop is only speeding up the inevitable. From now on in Turkey, "What's it to us what the American G.I.'s are doing in Vietnam?" is beside the point. Turks have put the ball back in the cart where it belongs. Either other scapegoats are found to account for U.S. addiction, or America finds a way to cure herself.

5. The Living Death of Junkie Augie Shulz

by Lois Wille

Do you remember what it was like, Augie Schulz, the day you enlisted in the Army?

It was your eighteenth birthday, and your dad was mad because you didn't wait to be drafted and your mom cried.

But you promised her you'd bring her back a fistful of medals, and you told your sisters not to worry: "The Commies won't last long with me over there."

That was nearly three years ago, and now you are ready for discharge. Waiting for the papers in the psychiatric ward of an Army hospital.

You won the medals, but you didn't win the war. You came home to show us our final great tragedy in Vietnam: our clean young men destroyed by heroin.

"I went in a nice middle-class kid wearing a suit," you say now. "And I came out a junkie."

Blue-eyed towhead, tall and lean—you could still pass for the ideal American golden boy. Except for that crazy earring and the dirty fatigue jacket and the sunken, blank eyes and the way you keep rubbing

Lois Wille is a feature writer for the Chicago *Daily News*.
Article © 1971 Chicago *Daily News*. Reprinted with permission.

your face and the constant pleading: "If I could just get my head straight . . ."

"He's a casualty, too," says his mother. "Some boys lose legs and arms. Augie lost his mind."

More than 5 million veterans of the Vietnam era have come home to us, but not the way their grandfathers came home after World War I, or their fathers after World War II, or their older brothers after Korea.

There are no parades for them, no hero's welcome.

They've come back with no legs, or blind, or back to a falling-apart city neighborhood and no job in sight. And instead of regaling admiring friends and neighbors with stories of bravery, they have to convince them they didn't kill babies.

They've come back raging with anger and frustrations at Allies who, they say, hate our guts.

And they tell you over and over, "The Vietnamese work for you during the day and shoot you in the back at night."

There are some who came back after building schools and fish hatcheries and bridges, who got to know and like the Vietnamese, who hope their good works will balance the slaughter. And prospective employers eye them curiously and ask, "You were in Vietnam—do you take drugs?" or "Don't you feel guilty about what you did over there?"

Now men like Augie Schulz are coming back to us, thousands of them. They didn't get the clean jobs. They killed—close, intimate, face-to-face killing, and it tore them apart.

"After a while, the more morbid it is the cooler you are," Augie says. "Like carving your name on somebody's chest while he's still alive, watching the funny looks on his face.

"I thought it would make a man out of me."

He enlisted in July 1968 and left behind a younger brother, seven younger sisters, his father, a crane operator in a steel mill, and his mother, a cashier in a dime store—all crowded into a cozy old gray shingle house in a Chicago suburb.

"It's falling apart, but it's home," says his mother, a warm, friendly woman trying hard to understand her son.

But his father, who drove a tank across Europe for General George S. Patton's Third Army in World War II, is disgusted.

"He won't even talk to me now," Augie says. "He says all war is bad. I try to tell him what this was like, but he won't listen."

What was it like, Augie? At first, dashing and handsome in his airborne uniform, newly arrived in the Mekong Delta and proud of his reconnaissance assignment with the Ninth Infantry Division, he was enthused about being a brave soldier.

It was dangerous. But that's what he wanted. That's why he quit high school, where, he said, "if you weren't a football hero or a brain, or didn't go around beating guys up, you were nobody."

But nothing had prepared him for the horror of the steaming jungles—the mutilated bodies bleeding in shallow streams, the smell of burning flesh, the sight of his best friend blowing up in front of him. "I had to sweep up the pieces," he wrote to his mother.

And the killing. The killing.

"When I first got there and saw what was going on, I didn't say anything," Augie says now. "They were older guys, and if you complain the guy you complain to could be a friend of the killer—and you could get a bullet in your back the next patrol.

"So after a while, you get used to it. You join in.

"Like, if we went into a village and saw somebody running and you felt like killing—you killed. And you'd say, 'Did you see the look on that gook's face when I shot him in the stomach?' "

Yet he did his job.

"The night before last I earned my first purple heart," he wrote to his mother in March 1969, two months after he arrived in Vietnam. "Don't worry. I just got some shrapnel in the face."

Later, there was another Purple Heart, and seven Air Medals for combat assault missions in helicopters, and a Bronze Star.

"I can't get over it—Sgt. Schulz," he wrote in April. "Groovie, huh?"

What kept him human, he said, was the children. There was an orphanage near his base for Vietnamese children whose parents were lost or killed in the war. Augie, with all those little sisters at home, loved them. Especially little Kimmie.

"She is seven years old, long black hair, and the cutest little smile I've ever seen," he wrote to his mother. "I'm getting papers to adopt her and take her back with me. Ma, you'll love her."

He bought clothes and toys for Kimmie, and spent his free time playing with her and her friends.

And then, in May, he wrote: "Kimmie is dead. Ma, it was terrible. You wouldn't want to know how she died, and I can't stand remembering."

Months later, when he came home for Christmas, he finally said to his mother, "Ma, you really want to know how Kimmie died?"

He had been on guard duty, he said, and there was a noise and a movement in the bushes. The guards yelled "Halt!" But the movement continued. They all fired.

Little Kimmie was found full of bullet holes. She had sneaked out of school to visit her friend while he walked guard.

"He told me they thought it was a Vietcong," Augie's mother says. "They all fired, but he blames himself. He said, 'I shot her, Ma—I killed her.' "

That summer, he learned about dope. First there was marijuana, and then opium. "We would get sticks about the size of a pencil," he says. "We'd shoot it, smoke it, eat it—fifty cents a stick. The Vietnamese sold it everywhere."

By this time, there was so much he wanted to forget.

"Ma, if I told you everything I done that is cruel here, you would never want to see me again," he wrote on June 29. "So it's best just to forget it as I will (I hope)."

Sometimes he wrote after smoking opium, and the letters were sickening—obscene, sometimes incomprehensible.

"I lost my favorite picture," he wrote to his mother. "The one with me eating Mother's Day dinner—C rations—on a pile of dead gooks. . . . You would really groove on it."

And, in September: "How are you? I'm fine, I guess—just totally confused but I'm almost always like that lately. . . . I get real spaced out and it takes a day or two to straighten out. I said to myself, 'Well, Aug, you gonna die here so ——— it all.' "

In November, when his year in Vietnam was nearly over, he volunteered for six more months there. He doesn't know exactly what tied him to the horror. It's all confused now in his mind.

He had a buddy who refused to carry a weapon, and he wanted to go back to protect him. He didn't want to leave the really good dope, the long dreamy days in the opium houses. And if he volunteered for six more months, he could go home early for a month's leave and have both Thanksgiving and Christmas there.

He hated Vietnam, the blood and violence, but something drew him back there.

The last six months were all downhill. "I had seen heroin, but I really didn't want to do it," Augie says. That's what everybody says about his first time with heroin.

He loved it, as they all do. And he became its slave, no longer a man—as they all do.

"I was being hassled all the time," he says, trying to explain why he took it. "They were keeping me in the rear as a guard. Everybody was afraid of me.

"There had been a few hand grenades landing in places they shouldn't have been—against the 'lifers' [career Army men]. And they blamed me.

"I had a number of busts for refusing to go into the field, to do any work. They gave me odd jobs like stringing barbed wire. I got busted down to permanent Private E-I. That's as low as you can get."

The heroin was cheap, and last spring it began showing up in great quantities. "You could pay for it by selling tires or radios," Augie says. "In my battalion, there were fifty of us junkies."

(Earlier in May the U.S. Army Provost Marshal's office in Saigon released a frightening study to an emissary of the House Foreign Affairs Committee. There are between 30,000 and 40,000 American serviceman in Vietnam addicted to heroin, the report said—more than one of every ten of our troops there. Some military authorities say this estimate is low.)

Finally, in July 1970, his time in Vietnam was up.

He stuffed his pockets with barbiturates so he could dull the heroin withdrawal on the flight home, and he came back.

"None of us could talk to him," says his pretty nineteen-year-old sister, Theresa. "I don't know what happened to him. He's had the same upbringing the rest of us had."

"He just got on my nerves so much," says his mother. "He contradicted himself so much. The little kids couldn't take his screaming and yelling. He slept all day and stayed out all night. Finally I said, 'Augie, if this is the way you're going to act I don't even want you here.' "

Last fall Augie spent three months in a psychiatric ward in Fitzsimmons Army Hospital in Denver. "We didn't get much care, except for a few who were really bad," he says.

In February a medical review board told him he was unfit for the Army, and awarded him a 30 percent psychiatric disability allotment. Later, this was reduced to 10 percent by Washington.

Since then, waiting for his discharge papers, Augie has spent his time at home fighting with his family, or crashing in various pads looking for dope, or sitting in the Chicago office of Senator Adlai E. Stevenson demanding a bigger disability allowance.

The only people who want to help him, he says, are the young radicals of the Chicago Area Military Project (CAMP), a group formed to foster dissent within the armed forces and provide legal aid for men and women in trouble with military law.

He talks vaguely about joining radical political groups, or working in a free medical clinic to help the poor, or joining a rural commune, or fighting in the streets for a new American revolution.

One minute he says he can't stand the sight of one more drop of blood, and the next he says he'll take up a gun anytime to fight here against "the pig oppressors."

"Mainly, I just want to get my head straight," he says.

Recently he went back to Fitzsimmons for more tests and his discharge papers.

He doesn't know what will happen to him. Neither does his family.

"My son Howie is fifteen now," says Augie's mother. "If this war is still on when he's eighteen, I'm sending him to Canada."

6. The Genocidal Fix: Washington

by Nellie Jo Lee

Any great city has contrasts, and should have. But in America's alabaster capital the scourge of heroin has made the contrasts so hauntingly cruel as to equal Kafka's worst nightmares. Take Capitol Hill, where the nation's lawmakers ostensibly attempt to weld personal interests, reelection, and the public good; the White House, where Richard Nixon attempts to reinsert the worst hallmarks of suburban banality into public life; HEW, where programs are formulated that don't offend anyone, but infuriate everyone. Cast starkly against all these elements of grand policy is an improbable, militant black man who goes by the title of Colonel Hassan and who spends his time scrounging up money to cure imponderable thousands of heroin addicts.

Some Washington officials ascribe a slight drop in the crime rate to Hassan's method of drug treatment. It includes the controversial ersatz heroin—methadone—for detoxification, *not* maintenance of the heroin habit. Initiated two years ago through Black-

Nellie Jo Lee, before escaping to the wilds of the Maine coast, worked for Antioch College and founded a newspaper. She now writes occasionally about the state of the culture. This article was specially prepared for this book.

man's Development Center, its strength is an unprecedented rehabilitation operation that includes drug education, crime prevention, and an ongoing job center. Blackman's Development Center operates as the community organization of Blackman's Volunteer Army of Liberation. A total of 196 full-time volunteers staff the methadone detoxification and rehabilitation program, along with an additional 400 volunteers recruited through a recent membership drive. There are 8,000 soldiers in Hassan's army; they direct their efforts at crime prevention, driving heroin out of Washington, and generally keeping the organization flourishing.

A riddle to most city officials, Hassan is the tall man in a black uniform who has treated 25,000 addicts since he began in June 1969. The city claims there are only an estimated 16,800 addicts in Washington. On the basis of the "official estimate" of 16,800 heroin addicts, two thirds of the addicts are under twenty-six years of age, 91 percent are black, 74 percent are male, and 52 percent began using heroin during the past four years. In one part of the inner city, it is estimated that 20 percent of boys from fifteen to nineteen and 38 percent of men from twenty to twenty-four years old are addicts. If the official estimates are correct, then Hassan knows most addicts personally. As a ghetto resident who once used heroin, sold wigs, and knows prison and street life from the inside, Hassan doesn't put anybody on when he maintains that there are at least 50,000 addicts in Washington.

The court system alone has sent him 2,500 addicts during the past year. "Out of 1,400 who lived within our structure, we've gotten complete cures," Hassan says. "We estimate 90 percent success." And he has the records to prove it, along with the names, addresses, and medical records of the other 25,000.

For decades heroin has been the plague of Washington's black community. As long as it was confined there, everything was all right to Middle America. No "crisis" existed until the children of the middle class were clutched in the addictive appeal of this powerful opium derivative that tends to numb the central nervous system. Now when heroin has transcended all cultural and racial barriers, everything is not all right. What racial implications and government guilt will do with the problem is no longer a matter of paradoxical rhetoric. Even the Bureau of Narcotics and Dangerous Drugs admits that at least 51 percent of all addicts today are white, against 44 percent in 1959. And the average age of the addict plunged from thirty-five in 1950 to twenty-three in 1970.

Now in the "crisis," the Feds have gleaned the results of a poshly funded, official methadone maintenance program. The fact that it reportedly brought a small dip in the D.C. crime rate influenced Nixon's decision to include rehabilitation funds in his anti-heroin package. Congress, meanwhile, has decided to provide more laws and money as Nixon proposes to set up "new machinery" to cope with addiction.

Though the bureaucrats won't admit it, Hassan

is certain that his massive inner-city program has strongly influenced administration action. Hassan has many critics among high-ranking city officials. And their charges that he operates in the "gray areas" of legality, is anti-Semitic, or doesn't have the appropriate number of doctors and nurses have lost him substantial funds from government and the local business community. "Maybe the government will listen one day," Hassan retorts. "Always we've had the problem that we had nothing—and we still have nothing. We're operating at a substantial deficit. We're spending twice as much as we ever got in government funds," he explains. His people have even gone into the exterminating and printing business.

Most of the officials making those charges never bothered to observe Hassan's operation in action. They never checked the expertise of his staff, nor did they check to see that his urinalysis equipment and laboratory operate as expediently as those with the most modern facilities. "Sure, these people may have sent their spies out here. But for all of their allegations, they've just sent the community people right to us."

When Hassan sharply disagrees with the methods government officials use to compile figures of drug addiction, he has every reason to be convinced that they don't do their homework carefully. Looking closely at the estimates on addiction, it becomes obvious that no one knows exactly what addiction means in this country. The National Institute of

Mental Health puts the overall national total of addicts at 250,000. But their top administrators admit the figure is "just a guess."

The process by which the "guess" is reached offers little reason for confidence. In 1970 about 900 persons died of drug overdoses in New York City, where half the country's addicts are thought to be. Some specialists believe that an estimate of the total number of addicts is obtained by multiplying annual overdose deaths by one hundred. That suggests at least 90,000 addicts in New York. Double that figure and there are 180,000 addicts for the country. Other "specialists" contend that the number of overdose deaths must be multiplied by 200 to obtain the total number of addicts. This would put the figure at 360,000 nationally. So the specialists compromise on their guesswork to round out the number at 250,000. Obviously the government isn't researching the problem by city block or any other way, except for guesswork on addicts who die. The only real figure in the lot of bureaucratic numbers is held by the Bureau of Narcotics and Dangerous Drugs; they have begun with the names of 60,000 known, registered addicts.

Summer on Capitol Hill is always a hot, air-conditioned affair. But over on 14th Street, N.W., the sun settles over the concrete and dirt like a sticky glob of chewing gum. It cuts through the ghetto, baring rows of grubby tenements, smelly garbage, and broken glass. The corner of 14th and V streets looks like most of the others that plague black people. This is where Whitey does not come, the place that makes him roll up his car windows and lock his doors when he does have to drive past.

On an ordinary afternoon in August, the corner is quiet. There is little movement except for the occasional slamming of a door. A D.C. cop car cruises down V Street. A small, thin black boy stands on the corner grinning up at a truck driver who has finished unloading an old washing machine.

"I want a quarter," the boy tells him. "Ain't you gonna give me a quarter?"

His mother comes down V Street, looking as gaunt and weary as the needle marks on her small dark arms. Her deep-set brown eyes are passive with the look of the habit she has scrounged to support for five years. At twenty-seven, she has three children. She works from early morning to noon as a waitress, then hustles in the afternoon and early evening to get enough money to sustain her habit. Taking the quarter from her son, she complains: "You'd better do more than that. You only got nine quarters today."

Her habit, like many others', depends upon theft and prostitution. Often the addict turns pusher when all else fails. The average habit costs $40 to $60 a day. The going price of street heroin is $10 a bag (confiscated street samples show the heroin content to be 5 percent—reasonably good stuff). In a week the cost of a habit like this could add up to $420, in a year to $22,000.

The Metropolitan Police Department (D.C.) reported 4,730 narcotics arrests during 1970—90 percent of these were related to heroin use or sale. Even at the terribly conservative estimate of 15,000 addicts in D.C., recent studies show that the estimated annual value of property and services transferred because of addiction through robbery, theft, prostitution, and drug sales is $328,100,100.

By night, this corner serves as a seedy, inner-city stage that has existed for years. First come the gaunt-faced prostitutes, young addicts hoping to turn a few tricks for enough bags (heroin) to last until morning. The pushers and the pimps are the nondescript, blank-faced ones. Their trick is turning bags and capsules for cash in the back alleys. But like one ex-pusher says: "They just put their profits right back into their arms."

Tight Bennie, a friend of the ex-pusher, comes on strong. He puts his situation right on the line: "Man, I had to split for a while. It was gettin' hot for me. These cops following me around . . . these crazy junkies all the time trying to steal my shit. Man, was I hot! I was doing so much jive with folks that I have to carry me two guns. You dig, man—like I got it knocked this time."

One of the dealers, Bennie pointed out, is a big tight-faced black man junkies call Fast Lonnie. "There's no mistaking this cat," Bennie says. "He cruises up and down the streets in a shiny red Eldorado."

Hassan estimates that there are at least 15 to 20 major dealers that operate in the city. He maintains that 80 percent of the heroin imported is done by the Mafia, with the Cosa Nostra and the New Syndicate responsible for the rest. Hassan has put quite a damper on the street scene. A large garage is plastered with posters. It strikes at "black-faced traitors who ride Eldorados and make your daughters into whores and prostitutes for the white drug suppliers." "Are you tired of being a prostitute? Are you tired of stealing from your mother, father, sister and brother?" demands another poster.

For almost two years the methadone detoxification and rehabilitation program operated as basically an outpatient setup at four centers. After treating more than 20,000 addicts on this basis, Hassan reduced his centers to two. He and his staff also operate three farms. "We can take sixty of seventy addicts a month to the farm and detoxify them." His interests are now directed toward a thirty-day "in-house" methadone detoxification program. Usually he has 125 addicts to a house, with a total capacity for treating 500 addicts.

"I am definitely opposed to a total methadone maintenance program as a way of handling the heroin problem," Hassan is quick to explain. "We run a detoxification program, *not* maintenance, with strong emphasis on educational therapy." The program's methodology is direct, specific, and without the hangups of most bureaucracies. He recognizes the need for a detoxification aspect for addicts who have reached the stage of no return. Methadone, once administered over a period of 60 days, has now been cut back to 30 days. It enables the addict to slowly and painlessly withdraw from heroin.

In providing rehabilitation and therapy, Hassan argues that the addict's fundamental problems are brought on by a lack of education, lack of job opportunities, and economic depravity: "All of these things have caused black people to use heroin. This also applies to whites from the other end of the spectrum."

The success of the programs of Blackman's Development Center is the chance for the addicted person to fortify himself to the point where he can lead his own life. Hassan admits his approach to therapy is in many ways a military one. "We teach the addict citizenship, the responsibility of the family," he explains. "The strength of this country has always been through the family, but the black man has never had it."

The Center's staff concentrates on teaching the addict to be self-sustaining and self-sufficient. Respect and the importance of wives and children are a priority. All education is aimed at equal participation in the community, to be able to produce their own food, their own clothing. An in-depth concentration on the powers and dangers of drugs to black people also leads the addict to the necessities of crime prevention in the community.

"As long as we can grow food on the farms to feed our own people, then we don't have to depend on it coming from other people," Hassan says, carefully pointing out that his people are not on welfare. "We do accept Medicaid because our people cannot afford the high costs or medicine and hospitals."

In some ghetto areas, it is rumored that the controversial drug methadone takes away manhood and softens the bones. But so far medical tests have not substantiated the claim.

Others charge that methadone is a white man's opiate, and some blacks say it is Whitey's tool for enslaving black people and other minority groups.

Colonel Hassan views "the methadone maintenance thing" as a simple institutional method for reducing crime.

When Hassan started using methadone as a way of detoxifying heroin addicts, many government officials were skeptical, yet curious. Though methadone, a synthetic opiate, does not in itself break addiction, it does ward off the social and economic effects of heroin. Methadone does block both the craving for heroin and the addict's ability to get high on it. No one quite understands the way it works, but its main attribute is to give the addict enough "stability" to hold a daily job. (In the nontolerant user, methadone can produce a high and lead to addiction. An addict, as in Hassan's detoxification program, builds up a gradual tolerance, which blocks the craving for heroin. After the addict builds up the tolerance, he may shoot up on heroin only to find that he doesn't get a high.)

The methadone maintenance approach, unlike Hassan's detoxification efforts, deals solely with the symptoms of heroin addiction. Its emphasis is not druglessness, but rather an attempt toward social rehabilitation for those addicts who cannot kick the habit by any other means. Most of those treated are volunteers. The balance are generally those referred by the courts or other formal agencies. Methadone in Washington has fairly good vibes within the "addict grapevine." One ex-addict admits: "The price of good stuff [about 8 percent heroin] has shot up. So a lot of junkies run to Hassan rather than run out there and risk getting caught." Some heroin dealers seem to have felt the crunch of Hassan's program, thereby forcing their pushers to run the "stuff" more openly to bring in the same profits. Some addicts are drawn to Hassan's program out of their own sense of weariness and futility. Says one, "I just couldn't steal anymore. It got so bad I was taking everything from my brothers."

Another who has used both drugs sums up the difference between methadone and heroin: "With heroin you nod . . . you get very drowsy . . . you just want to go off in your own corner. There's no end, you get no tolerance. You shoot five bags [heroin]; if there's no high you shoot four more. Then you get dried out and you just have to start all over again. On methadone you just take your steady dose . . . and that's it. You can function like other people."

Many of Hassan's critics confuse Blackman's Development Center [detoxification and rehabilitation program] with Blackman's Volunteer Army of Liberation. Often whites are skeptical when they consider his army of 8,000 black soldiers. "Blackman's Army" often becomes "black militants" to those who do not know its purpose. The army has had two goals since its founding in 1966: to fight crime in the black community and to drive out heroin. One of the Army's first principles is that the fight against drugs, crime, and the exploitive relations that destroy the quality of life must come from within the community at a grass-roots level. Hassan maintains that the police are doing about all they can.

When Hassan formed his first centers, he had already determined a number of his priorities through the goals of his Volunteer Army. They were first directed at cleaning up slum neighborhods and giving food, housing, and clothing to poor families. But he increasingly came to see drugs as the real blight in the community. Self-defense was the first concern: "I tell my people that Whitey hasn't lost a war yet. But in the unhappy event that a race war starts, we will be there." His next priority was self-help: "Civil rights leaders raise a lot of hell. But they don't do anything. When they're gone, there's no one left. In an army, there's always someone to take your place."

Hassan's centers operate under three basic premises: all patients are former heroin users; all methadone is consumed at the Center in the presence of staff; all weapons are left at the door.

The Volunteer Army has had an incredible and

rocky growth pattern: "In June of 1966, forty men met together to form the Army, electing me commander-in-chief. Three months later we were down to one person. Five months later we had two members." Since 1965, the Army has had a phenomenal growth throughout the country. Printed brochures and articles distributed by the organization have undoubtedly helped to spread the word. "We now have eight thousand soldiers in the army," Hassan relates. "Currently we also have offices in Columbus and Dayton, Ohio. We'll be opening up in Atlanta before summer is gone. Then Los Angeles, Denver, and Newark."

Hassan and the Army have had to use "other" ways to get at the drug problem, including occasional visits to dealers. Sometimes a visit may be just a personal warning, delivered by Hassan and two or three of his officers. They just go into the dealer's house or store and tell him he's "got to stop." If that doesn't work, there is a sterner version of the visit. A door may get kicked in and a few people may get punched in the mouth. But the drugs in the place are completely confiscated and destroyed.

Colonel Hassan was never a novice where drugs were concerned. Born Albert "Tony" Osborne, he has often riddled those city leaders who are sometimes skeptical about his past. During his forty-seven years, he's known the ins and outs of training schools, prisons, and the streets. His ventures as a wig salesman brought him to many realities. But the thing that Hassan knew as well as or better than anyone else was the pain and weariness that guts a person on heroin. He had used heroin himself back in 1941. By the time the riots broke out in the sixties, no one had to tell him where it was at: "I saw girls I went to school with. They were totally destroyed by drugs and prostitution."

The things that an addict must do to maintain even a $50-a-day habit are so debasing as to remove almost all hope of beating it. Over the addict's head is the constant threat: either find more money or suffer the exhausting, painful trauma of withdrawal. The answer is clear enough: keep on hustling and stealing in an endless pressure-cooker existence. For heroin's brief euphoria and the relief from tension and sick withdrawal symptoms, the addict pays an excruciating price, always on the fringes of death from disease and infection, induced by improperly cleaned needles. Addicts have been known to die immediately after a self-administered intravenous injection, with only edema of the lungs found at autopsy.

Hassan confronts the addict every day. It is an unending job that demands his full attention: how to find enough money to keep his people going; what to do with the endless number of weary black and white addicts who find their way to his door. Hassan, who sometimes appears bitter in the face of his critics, probably holds more compassion for their ignorance than anything else. How does he really feel?

"It's really low down . . . such a good feeling to know I've finally kicked in with something that's doing good to help people. It does me good when the government shuts off funds; it just brings the people to us."

7. Drug Law History Politics and Prohibition

by Maxine Kenny

America is a consumer society. Many of its consumers indulge in one "habit" or another—and American businesses, both "legitimate" and "illegitimate," push products to meet the demand they help to create. Whether it be a housewife who turns to Librium to help her get through another tense or boring day in the suburbs, or a black teen-ager copping a fix on the corner in an urban slum, the scene is similar—if you have the money, you can get "relief." But the recent penetration of "hard" drugs into middle-class society, as well as the fear of addiction-related crime against property in "good" neighborhoods, has set up a public outcry which is reverberating in the mass media and the legislative halls. Since the early sixties, politicians from urban areas have been under pressure from their constituents to find more effective ways to sweep the addicts (i.e., the nonwhite burglars, the muggers, the thieves) off the streets. Nelson Rockefeller based his 1966 campaign for the governorship of New York on a civil commitment program which was called "treatment" to assuage the

Maxine Kenny is a member of the radical Health Policy Advisory Center in New York City. Reprinted with permission from *Health/Pac Bulletin* (June 1970).

reformer conscience, but in reality merely made it easier to pick up more addicts and put them away for longer periods of time without burdening the courts. In 1965, John Lindsay pointed to addiction as a serious problem, and partly on the basis of his promise to do something about it, he was elected mayor of New York. Richard Nixon picked up the popular theme emanating from New York and, after campaigning successfully on a "law and order" platform, in the fall of 1969 submitted a "get tough on pushers" drug-control bill to Congress.

Such political appeals to the public's fear of addicts and addiction are an attempt to capitalize on what the newspapers call a growing "epidemic." There are an estimated 300,000 heroin addicts in this country. U.S. heroin addiction rates have climbed faster than in any other Western country. In the last twenty years, the number of known addicts has increased 300 percent. *Forbes* magazine states the magnitude of the problem in business terms: "It's an industry that runs to nearly three billion dollars a year in the U.S. alone. . . . It's a real growth industry, expanding in the U.S at ten percent or more yearly." The U.S. addiction rate is thirty times that of Italy, Belgium, Russia, Poland, and Brazil; ten times that of Britain and France; and twice that of Canada. (In the early sixties, the census of addicts in any given European country rarely exceeded 500 individuals. It is possibly of some social significance that the severest drug problem in European history was recorded in pre-World War II Germany, which saw a phenomenal growth in addiction to hard drugs. By the time the war commenced, there were at least 10,000 known German addicts.)

The white middle class's increasing concern over addiction comes not merely from the growth in addiction, but from the fear of being victimized by the same drug evils that have plagued the ghetto communities for years. Not only might ghetto addicts boldly venture into the white community to steal goods to support their habit, but middle-class teenagers are getting hooked on readily available heroin. The ensuing publicity and concern has all but obliterated the fact that black and brown communities are still the primary victims of drug addiction. Most drug-related crime, involving an estimated $15 billion in property loss each year, is still committed in the ghetto. Notwithstanding, the fears of the white middle class have increased, and the poor communities have been placed in double jeopardy by the "law and order" campaigns of politicians which reinforce an already repressive police force.

Now the fear of violence in the white middle-class community has given way to another fear: addiction itself has penetrated some of its most coveted institutions—suburban schools and business and industry (even so, 75 percent of addicts are from minority groups). Alarmed parents in such places as Smithtown, Long Island, Clifton, New Jersey, and Grosse Point, Michigan, are insisting that school officials give their children saliva, blood, or urine tests to determine what drugs they are using. Even big business is worried. Last fall sixty top business executives who make up the Commerce and Industry Association devoted their annual meeting to learning how to recognize addiction among their junior execs. And in the spring of 1970, top officials of the UAW admitted concern about reports of widespread use of narcotics in the plants.

Confronted by an alarmed, middle-class public, most politicians are adopting a modified line about addiction: the Establishment is shifting the onus of criminality from the drug user to the drug pusher, while searching frantically for a medical "fix" with which to treat the victim. Even President Nixon, who as recently as the summer of 1969 was calling for increased punishment of drug users, has realized such laws can be applied to the sons and daughters of his own constituents (and, in any event, have proven unsuccessful). After due consideration, he said in a message to Congress the fall of 1969: "It has been a common oversimplification to consider narcotics addiction or drug abuse to be a law enforcement problem only." But Nixon is a mere upstart compared to New York's Governor Rockefeller when it comes to blowing with the wind. The same Rocky who in 1967 ran unabashedly on a "sweep the addicts off the streets of New York" platform told a conference on drug abuse in 1970: "Curing addiction is one of the toughest jobs in our society. It would be a tragedy if there were those who tried to make political gain from the suffering and degradation of narcotics addiction."

New York City's Mayor Lindsay has also gained considerable political mileage from the drug crisis. Just before the primaries in 1969, Lindsay announced the formation of a Federal-City Narcotics Enforcement Task Force in a joint news conference with U.S. Attorney General Mitchell. The task force still doesn't exist. Then in October 1969, just days before election day, Lindsay joined Senators Javits and Goodell in calling for a "moonshot" war on drugs and requesting $1.5 billion in federal funds for a five-year program. Even though the money didn't arrive from Washington, Lindsay announced the appointment of Robert Morgenthau to the newly created post of third deputy mayor. Morgenthau, a crimebusting former U.S. District Attorney, was assigned to clean up the drug problem in February 1970. Lindsay established a City Narcotics Control Commission and made Morgenthau the chief. In March, the new third deputy mayor announced his candidacy for the Democratic nomination for governor. And in April, just two and a half months after the fanfare of another call for a total war on drugs, Morgenthau retired to run for the Democratic nomination for governor, using the drug problem as a major campaign issue. The office of third deputy mayor was phased out.

Many politicians are beginning to pay lip service to the plight of the addict-victim, and a smaller number are fighting for increased appropriations for the treatment of addiction. But they are up against all the problems left by a fifty-year history of laws which force addicts to become criminals. All forms of addiction, though rooted in the social experience of individuals, are shaped in part by society's attitude toward addiction and by the controls it imposes. In America (and through America's influence, in much of Asia) the use of "hard" drugs was prohibited in the early part of the twentieth century. In so doing, society forced the addict to become a criminal to survive. Moreover, if he were part of an oppressed minority group, he might actually be attracted to this one facet of the economy which was "open" and offered opportunity. And if he were a successful hustler, he might gain considerable respect among his peers. In most European countries, by contrast, where addiction to "hard" drugs was viewed as just another medical problem with a prescribed treatment, such a drug subculture never gained momentum. The "British system," for example, merely authorized physicians to write prescriptions for heroin. Recently an unprecedented jump in addiction prompted the British to switch from self-administered drugs to a more formal system of clinic dispensaries. Whether the recent increase in addiction is attributable to Britain's "liberal" policy regarding addiction or whether it has other social bases is presently being debated.

The prohibitionist attitude toward drugs which led to this country's law enforcement approach to drug addiction has its roots in the last half of the nineteenth century. Drug addiction was growing at home. "Soldiers' sickness," or addiction to morphine, afflicted more than 45,000 Civil War veterans as a result of the liberal administration of the painkiller on the battlefield. By the end of the war, many others had taken to opium smoking, which had been introduced by the Chinese who emigrated to the United States during the 1850's and 1860's. Though many continued to think of opium smoking as strictly an Oriental sport, more than half the imported opium reached the general market. At the same time, a flourishing patent medicine industry found that a touch of opium or morphine could ease almost any pain—and, coincidentally, sell a lot of bottles of medicine. As America turned the corner of the twentieth century authorities estimated there were at least 100,000 addicts to morphine, opium, and heroin.

The discovery of the drug addiction problem around the turn of the century coincided historically with the campaign to rid the nation of another scourge—alcohol. Both the general prohibitionist sentiment of the era and a specific collection of men in the Treasury Department who were charged with the enforcement of the Volstead Act were influential in labeling the addict a criminal. The American delegation attending the first International Opium Convention at The Hague in 1912 pushed very strongly for international drug controls. When no such controls could be agreed on, the delegation returned home determined to clean up its own backyard. The United States made her first stab at controlling the flow of narcotics in 1914 by passing the Harrison

Act. The law itself is a relatively mild-mannered and innocuously worded revenue measure. But its subsequent interpretation and the attached severe penalties set America apart from most other Western countries. (Interestingly, the "nonprohibitionist" British narcotics control measure passed in 1920 is almost identical to the Harrison Act.)

On the face of it, the Harrison Act simply requires that persons and firms importing and handling drugs register and pay a nominal tax fee. The Act went on to say that addicts who had previously purchased drugs from pharmacies and mail order houses must henceforth obtain their drugs from a physician. The portion of the law which was open to interpretation, however, was the section that said a physician could dispense drugs only in the course of legitimate practice. What constituted "legitimate" practice? A series of Supreme Court rulings from 1915 to 1922 said: first, that possession of a smuggled drug (i.e., one on which the tax had not been paid) was a crime; second, that a doctor could not prescribe drugs to "satisfy the craving" of an addict, but only for purposes of withdrawal; and, finally, that the only circumstance under which a doctor could prescribe drugs for withdrawal was for an addict under institutional care. For all practical purposes, since by 1922 there were no longer any hospitals which would treat addicts, all legal access to drugs had been foreclosed.

The enforcement of the Harrison Act was initially placed in the hands of internal revenue collectors in the Treasury Department. But in 1919 the agents charged with this responsibility were thrown into a newly created Prohibition Unit along with the agents who were to enforce the newly enacted Volstead Act. The Treasury Department's drug control regulations which were issued in 1921 were based on the Supreme Court decisions and bore the definite stamp of the prohibition mongers. Their influence is most starkly reflected in the fact that 44 narcotic-dispensing government clinics which had been opened in 1919 under the reign of Internal Revenue Service were summarily ordered closed in 1920 by the prohibition commissioner.

Legally, medical alternatives to the "law and order" interpretation of the Harrison Act were still not ruled out. Had anyone chosen to challenge the Court's early decisions and the ensuing federal regulations, a Supreme Court decision handed down in 1925 might have served as an opening wedge. The case involved Dr. Charles Linder from Seattle; unlike the doctors in the earlier cases who were involved in prescribing rather large quantities of drugs, he supplied only four pills, to be used for withdrawal, to an informer posing as an addict. The Court cleared Dr. Linder of charges, described addiction as a disease, and said that a physician acting in good faith could give drugs for withdrawal. But instead of spurring reform, the Linder incident—which cost the doctor more than $30,000 and a two-year loss of license—probably did more to ensure that doctors would stay clear of addicts. After all, they reasoned, bad publicity—whether you win or lose—could cost a man his career.

Organized medicine—through the voice of the American Medical Association (AMA)—was less than valiant when it came to fighting for the health and welfare of addicts. But it is probably safe to say that their attitudes were a fair reflection of the attitude of the medical profession in general. They not only willingly acquiesed to the Treasury Department regulations, but wholeheartedly endorsed the closing of the government drug clinics. Picking up on the rhetoric of the prohibitionists, a spokesman for the AMA said in 1921:

> The shallow pretense that drug addiction is a disease which the specialist must be allowed to treat, which pretended treatment consists in supplying its victims with the drug which has caused their physical and moral debauchery . . . has been asserted and urged in volumes of literature by self-styled specialists. . . . The vice that causes degeneration of the moral sense, and spreads through social contact, readily infects the entire community, saps its moral fiber, and contaminates the individual members one after another like the rotten apples in a barrel of sound ones.

Until the late fifties, the AMA consistently and vehemently opposed all "ambulatory methods of treatment of drug addiction, whether practiced by the private physician or by the so-called 'narcotics clinic' or dispensary."

Though organized medicine opted out on its responsibility to treat the addict, the federal Public Health Service lent medical respectability to the federal addiction program by setting up federal "hospitals" to get the addicts off the streets in the thirties. Procedures for criminal and civil involuntary commitments were adopted. The treatment centers which are in Forth Worth, Texas, and Lexington, Kentucky, were traditionally long on detention and short on treatment. Even their own statistics reveal that fewer than 3 percent of their "graduates" have been "cured."

From the twenties to the fifties, lawyers showed as little interest in protecting the addict's legal rights as did the doctor in considering his health rights—and for many of the same financial reasons. Narcotics laws as defined by the Treasury Department and enforced by the Bureau of Narcotics (established within the department in 1930) until very recently made little distinction between the perpetrator of the crime and the victim of it. And in practical terms, the victim received the harsher treatment of the two—both at the hands of the police and in the courts. Given the choice of an addict or a peddler to defend, the lawyer is more likely to choose the man who can pay. Records show that higher courts spend a disproportionate amount of time on the constitutional rights of traffickers (illegal search and seizure cases), rather than on the same constitutional rights of addicts which may have been abused.

Before 1930 and the creation of the Bureau of Narcotics in the Treasury Department, addiction was considered a federal concern almost exclusively. The newly formed Bureau quickly sought the cooperation of the states in an effort to fill possible gaps in the law. Most states responded by adopting a suggested Uniform Narcotics Law which was similar to the Harrison Act, although many of the penalties, which varied from state to state, were often even harsher. Many of the state laws added marijuana in the list of dangerous narcotics. The federal law which authorized the establishment of Lexington and Fort Worth hospitals in 1929 also defined marijuana as a "habit-forming narcotic drug." With the way paved, the federal government passed a Marijuana Tax Act (similar to Harrison) in 1937.

The laws remained pretty much intact until the 1951 Kefauver hearings on organized crime triggered a public outcry for increased punishment for those involved in the drug scene. Congress passed the Boggs Amendment, which instituted minimum penalties for all drug crimes. Possession of drugs and selling them were treated similarly: the penalties ranged from two to five years for a first offense, from ten to twenty years for a third offense. As before, many of the states passed similar "Little Boggs Acts." In 1956 the Congress passed the Narcotic Drug Control Act. This time possession and sale were distinguished, and minimum penalties were upped. Possession alone could net a prisoner anywhere from two to forty years, depending upon whether it was a first or third offense. The sale of narcotics to a person under eighteen could mean anywhere from ten years to death. And once again the states followed suit by passing similar drug control acts of their own.

The agency assigned to enforce the drug laws—the Bureau of Narcotics and Dangerous Drugs (it was renamed and moved from the Treasury Department to the Department of Justice in 1968)—has enthusiastically capitalized on the "signs of the times." Because it has a large public relations budget, and controls most information on narcotics which is disseminated on the federal level, it is able to produce data to show effectiveness or establish need. The Bureau—though it failed to produce credible statistical data regarding either its own enforcement activities or the dimensions of the domestic addiction problem—has been highly critical of nonrepressive systems of treatment. When reformers appeared to be gaining ground in the mid-fifties, the Bureau took it upon itself to widely circulate a report which debunked Britain's medical approach to addiction. The Bureau concluded that the British system was little different from ours and any difference in the size of the addict population was attributable to the fact that the British are not "addiction-prone."

Herbert Anslinger, an ex-Prohibition officer, who headed the Bureau from its inception until 1962, was a J. Edgar Hoover-type figure who was not beyond appealing to the political fantasies of Congress when appropriation time came around. During the Cold War, he convinced Congress that the spread of addiction in America was a "Commie plot"—that even the combined efforts of the U.S. Army, Air Force, and Navy would have a difficult time stopping the influx of dangerous drugs. Of course, he promised, an increased budget for the Bureau of Narcotics would be a step in the right direction.

Since 1960 there has been a general reappraisal of the harsh punishment of drug users, although the "reappraisal" has been more rhetoric than reality. In 1962 the two states with the greatest narcotics problem in the U.S., New York and California, followed in the footsteps of the federal government, which had set up civil commitment procedures for Lexington and Fort Worth in the thirties, and instituted state civil commitment programs. Because these federal and state programs are billed as "rehabilitation," not as "punishment," the addicts committed to such institutions are often denied even basic constitutional rights—e.g., it is only recently that the courts required a jury trial before commitment in New York.

In 1970 New York City followed in the footsteps of the federal and state moves to restrict the addict by instituting what was in effect a compulsory treatment program for the addict's "own good." The City Department of Social Services issued an administrative order which denied public assistance to an addict unless he was in treatment or a definite treatment commitment was agreed to. Commissioner of Social Services Jack Goldberg claimed the city was looking for a better return on its $5.7 million per year which goes to a minimum of 6,000 addicts.

Goldberg assured critics that "the junkie will be exposed to a whole series of treatment programs." But there are already waiting lines for all the treatments (effective or ineffective) that exist in the city. What is more likely to happen is that these addicts will find themselves in "treatment" in the prison-like state narcotic rehabilitation centers which have been operating at 25 percent below capacity.

At the federal level, officials are trying to capitalize on the political potential of the drug issue, and respond accordingly. In 1969, Nixon's newly appointed head of the Bureau of Narcotics and Dangerous Drugs, Robert Ingersoll, sensing the Congress was shifting toward waging war on the pushers while relaxing the penalties on drug users (since many of their sons and daughters were being picked up on dope charges), told a congressional committee: "Our major concern is with [drug traffic's] criminal aspects. . . . A greater effort will be expended now and in the future to apprehend and prosecute major drug traffickers and also to prevent violation of the drug and narcotic laws, especially among the young, the naïve, and ordinarily law-abiding public." Congress granted his request for a program of training and staffing foreign narcotics posts, an incentive plan to persuade foreign growers to stop producing opium, substantial increases in border guards and agents for both federal and local narcotics bureaus, and increased research and education into the drug problem. The Bureau's estimated 1971 budget, $34.5

million, almost double that of 1969, reflected the administration's stepped-up spending for drug law enforcement.

In his first major statement on drug addiction in the summer of 1969, President Nixon took a hard line. Among other provisions, Nixon recommended that marijuana use be treated as a felony. This put lead in his trial balloon, and Nixon liberalized the plan under heavy criticism from such men as Senator Gaylord Nelson, who said, "It is heavy on policing and weak on rehabilitation." Subsequently, the White House bill was incorporated into the Dodd bill.

Meanwhile, back in New York State many legislators in Albany were aghast in the spring of 1970 when the appropriations bank was broken and the legislative session was drawing to a close, and Governor Rockefeller announced a $265 million "declaration of total war" against drug abuse by those under sixteen. It was the year of concern for the teen-age addict—and Rocky, up for reelection, knew a good issue when he saw one. Many Democratic legislators from New York City made a counter "declaration" that Rocky's "war" was a hoax. Nevertheless, Rocky's call for the legislature to trim $64 million from other programs so it could be made available on a fifty-fifty matching basis to localities—localities which would find it next to impossible to raise cash for teen-age drug programs—was heeded. It would have been political suicide for critics to do otherwise. The remaining $200 million of the Rockefeller "war," for construction or leasing of facilities for youth treatment centers, was to be provided by state housing bonds to provide loans to local governments. But the lion's share of Rocky's war made headlines, then disappeared.

The much publicized shift in public policy toward addicts—from one of punishment to one of treatment—will probably not mean much to most addicts. Even though the penalty for "possession" has been eased, it will mainly benefit those who can afford to buy their drugs and do not have to push to make money to support their habits, as is the case with most lower-class addicts. It is true that there are now many in the medical profession who are willing to treat addicts. Even the AMA, which for decades supported a "law and order" line, came full circle last winter when it declared: "Drug-dependent persons should be treated as patients rather than criminals." But little money is available for "treatment"; most of the effort still goes to repression. Moreover, in the past, "treatment" has most commonly been nothing more than a euphemism for imprisonment. Finally, really meaningful treatment means changing the conditions which lead to addiction. Even if a medical "cure" for addiction were found tomorrow, poor people would still lack meaningful employment, decent housing, good schools, etc.; the conditions that generate addiction would remain untouched.

8. The Political Economy of Junk

by Sol Yurick

Tragedy of the kid junkie? How? Do it like Time-LifeHamillDailyUSNews&WorldReportBreslin. . . . Say something about the eyes. Coldness in the eyes; tombstones in the eyes of a pinkcheeked kid who's caught a Jones. Wan face. The shivers on a hot day and sweating on a cold one. Do the desolation row bit. Relate to bombed-out houses; war image. Crouching in the rotted doorway and living in the abandoned slum building. OD's in the empty rooms far away from mama. Even highschool football heroes are on scag. Middle-class addiction, so therefore it is now *tragedy*. What was the daily body-count before it moved into middle America? Junkies in Larchmont and Scarsdale and Riverhead and Croton and Greenwich, don't forget those. Put in a touch about the hypodermic, the works in a hardtop cigarette pack. Mention hepatitis. Picture an arm, fisted and knot-muscled and the needle in; the plunger rising and falling, the blood sucking in and out, mixing with the stuff, the taut raised vein

Sol Yurick is a Marxist critic and author of three novels: *The Warriors*, *Fertig*, and most recently, *The Bag*. Article © by Sol Yurick, 1970. First published in *Monthly Review* (December 1970).

before the boot comes . . . and how some get erections and orgasms. . . . The kid pusher. And, oh yes, don't forget the faces. Maybe something about the faces, like Jewish kids about to be incinerated. Ah, that's a good touch. Junk has made them all tragic-looking. And do the thing about the kidgirl prostitutes to whom come the fat-ankled businessmen and bored diplomats tooling down Flatbush Avenue in ticket-immune Cadillacs while cops a block away hassle long-haired kids. And the rise and fall of the market. They all talk about prices and the weight. Jazz about the slums. Slick look of the hard sixteen-year-old pusher, cool and sadistic and liplicking, holding the product off the market for twenty minutes more, with his plea-faced entourage of the junk-starved: there's nothing like humiliation transmitted downward and inward to break down old hangups and loyalties till shame is banal and guilt not even a memory. Oh yes, bring in some heroic social worker fighting against the odds. And the tough-minded social scientist ready to tread on a few toes. Little idiosyncratic touches: the stockbroker on cocaine. . . . And how high-level executives in New York Life and Chase Manhattan. . . . Maybe it's not so idiosyncratic after all. . . .

But tragedy submitted to economics becomes comedy for anyone with a strategic and long-range outlook. Even *Oedipus* is impossible without its initiating economic crisis; and the tragic hero (or antihero) reflects a specific historical and social fate, not a psychological one. After all, if one wants the exact *feel* of it, the sufferings of the junkie, the heroic and bitter struggle to kick, the recidivism, the rest of it, Nelson Algren's *Man with the Golden Arm* is still the last word.

The addict, no matter what his psychological perceptions about himself, no matter what theorizing psychiatrists do, is a social type generated in response to changes in the social economy in a time of world crisis. A mistake frequently made is to view drug consumption merely as an indulgence, a gratification, an escape rather than a market response to economic and social dislocation. Under capitalism, large combinations struggle to evolve and, through control of product and marketing techniques, determine through what channels need shall be directed to feed. In a pressure-to-consume world, *all* pleasures can be made addictive: and the important thing to remember is that the *head*, intoxication, is a need, and needs can be channeled into markets which can relate satisfaction to product, in fact make gratification impossible without an attendant product. The addiction that has a built-in accelerative velocity and promotes a high rate of turnover is ideally profitable.

A little arithmetical probe: 500,000 junkies (I speak of junkies alone, but drug consumption should not be broken down into consumption of types and kinds of drugs: at this point in history it is one unified and contiguous market), an extremely modest estimate, spending $20 a day on their habit ($150-a-day habits are not unknown) add up to a market of more than three and a half *billion* dollars a year. (*Business Week* estimates three billion dollars a year.) Therefore, it's not a matter of psychology, individual variation, individual choice, tragedy, if you will: specific individuals may avoid that specific fate, but growing numbers of people cannot avoid becoming addicts. (Put another way: what's the effect on the personality of *not* having a car in Los Angeles?) The junkie shivering in the doorway, a picture image-hungry reporters seem addicted to, is better understood in terms of his single-minded and back-breaking contribution to the Gross National Product. Can this state be undesirable then?

This is a time, especially in the last two administrations, when it has become necessary for our economy to expand in forced marches, and this has created unbearable tensions. There is a need now for a new kind of labor force, always available, trainable and retrainable, mobile and readily allocable, a kind of army, really, yet retaining channels of opportunity and advancement for the fittest who are successful in the competitive free-enterprise market. This has created a series of dislocations which are perceived, personally, on the level of restlessness, of despair, of neurosis, psychosis, of shrinkage of available and traditional roles, and the growth of new, unbearable ones, the reluctant dropping off of the outmoded values and obsolescent loyalties.

Given this time when major institutions are breaking down (as they should and must, eroding inefficient and counterproductive relations, freeing, as it were, a frozen and static ideological capital), when enormous enforced population shifts have created what is now known as the crisis of cities, when basic social relations, particularly those relating to marriage and sex, are being devalued (and women, who by demanding rights with disastrous economic implications, are on the verge of adding to the major crisis by defining themselves as equal on the market, or worse, even defining their very housework and childbearing roles—claiming that their very sexual juices lubricate the wheels of industry—as contributory to economic well-being), when legal institutions are overloaded and cannot function smoothly, generating disrespect that has malfunctional and disruptive potentialities, when the modes and vehicles of public communication and service are breaking down because major priorities lie, for the time being, in the defense sector, we are in the midst of a crisis of superstructure.

These tensions are most transmitted to the young, who are, economically, a deprived, one may even say a parasitic, grouping with certain elements of unified class interest which have been defined for them by mass media education. The first results of this disruption have been felt in the schools, creating further problems for industry as the population reservoir for further recruitment is threatened with dysfunction and infection creating an area of potential *revolution.* (It must be understood that the grouping being drawn most heavily to heroin is youth. To be sure there is a vast population of older addicts—

alcohol and drugs—but a great number are not even aware they are addicts. Most of these addicts already have a work habit and an investment in ongoing society. It's not this segment of the population we're talking about.) It is the *young*, as will be shown, for whom drug-economic therapy is most indicated.

How then, to prevent the fabric of society from becoming completely unraveled, does one achieve a reintegration of confidence, a restoration of the faith to fight off internal threats to economic and ideological world goals? How does one retranslate what is a failure of confidence in one mode of productive activity into confidence in a new mode of economic behavior, achieving, at the same time, a tractable labor force, still permitting the rising-expectations syndrome to find outlets for enterprise on the part of those growingly vast segments of the population who are, for all practical purposes, irrelevant?

How does one allow for the rise of new elites whose energies might otherwise be destructive if frustrated?

What product, or set of products, what set of economic relations tends, more than others at this particular time in history, to foster those aims and further the historical development of capitalism, proving to the world at large its fecund viability?

Only the imaginative use of drugs—especially heroin—fulfills these conditions which call for a vast acceleration of what only the most conservative would call the *illegal* labor force.

It has been our naïve tendency to regard the legal sector as separated and contradictory to the illegal, just as we tend to think of negative numbers as opposed to positive numbers, failing to understand that all numbers, like legality and illegality, are *not* opposed, but part of one system. Traditionally, capitalism has developed to its commanding world position by working the whole range. Heightened illegal activity is both a response to an expanding economy and a mode of keeping options open for the creation of new capital and new capitalists. The rise in drug consumption is better understood if we regard the matter as a political and economic subsystem contiguous with the rest of the social economy; it is a model of imperfect competition and uneven development, *laissez-faire* on the bottom and monopolistic on the top. The junkie's hand is not so much raised against society; rather he is involved in on-the-job training in a true street academy: certainly, for the ghetto dweller, pushing, purchasing, and habit-resolution (the fix) may be his salvation, redeeming him for the market and thus society.

Further, in our panic, we fail to remember the historic role of intoxicants in general, and opium in particular, as a civilizing force, one of the many adjuncts for the creation of capital, useful as well for the opening of rigid, closed societies to market conditions. Intoxicants break down counterproductive, counterconsumption, ritual customs where other educative (even forceful) means have failed: intoxicants are deconditioners and decustomizers. Specifically, while we all remember now the role of liquor in winning the long march against the Indians, we tend to forget its usefulness in keeping struggling pioneers on the job, settling the frontier when they were unable, in their short-sightedness, to perceive the dictates of Manifest Destiny. Inhuman jobs, such as clearing and settling the land by hand, became bearable while drunk. Votes have been traditionally purchased by drink. Britain in the eighteenth century deliberately consumed surplus wheat as gin consumed by surplus labor.

We also forget, for instance, that China was opened to the West by control of opium, for which some very hard little wars were fought, and that many British and American fortunes (one calls to mind the Peabodys, the Cabots, the Delanos) were based on the opium trade. We fail to recall that such world leaders as Chiang Kai-shek got his start as a member of the underworld in Shanghai dealing in, among other things, opium. So valuable is this raw material that vast opium fields of Burma and Laos and Vietnam are still controlled by elements of the Kuomintang who deal through Taiwan and American middlemen. Nor must we overlook the role of Air America (a CIA airline) in flying opium runs out of Laos; Marshal Ky (then Colonel) took fliers in this market. There are those who will demur at the idea that the CIA may be, among their other graces, pushers, or that American Indochinese policy is concerned with skag. But, as pointed out, when main-chance opportunities are closed, advancement too slow, people in key positions will not only find ingenious modes of success, but will find ways of using their strategic levers of power to move even national policy.

Nor can we forget that morphine, opium, heroin, cocaine, have been traditionally used in the South: one has only to remember the lumber and turpentine camps of some years ago. Furthermore, the use of intoxicants, sometimes disguised as medicine, has been most helpful in keeping farmers' wives productive and on the job, producing a labor force, contributing to the vital agricultural industry in that time of transition before most of the lands were ready to be passed on to the more efficient and rationalized agribusinesses. In fact the full story of the intoxication of women has yet to be written. South American Indians are kept productive at labor-intensive jobs by chewing coca leaves, from which cocaine is made. We manage to function beautifully with an extraordinary level of intoxication among leading political types, to say nothing of the business executive class, but then, the role of civilizing the world is not an easy one and there are periods in history when individuals must sacrifice themselves for the future: you don't make an omelet without breaking a few eggs.

Operation Intercept heralded what was in fact a great leap forward, and its architect was Nixon. What was instituted was a kind of protective tariff, carried out another way, in favor of heroin. This was implemented all over the country on the local level by a stepped-up war against marijuana pushers, but a relaxation of the struggle against the heroin pushers, who could be seen working in the summer streets unmolested. Kids themselves made the analysis that Nixon was trying to hook them onto bad stuff: why they were not able to resist will be discussed later. Of course it should be understood that aside from its other implications, marijuana is a much cheaper product and less profitable than heroin. But what was most dangerous about marijuana use was the potentially disruptive *mystique* of its community of users, and communalists consume much less than isolated individuals. Grassblowers *give* one another presents of love: smack heads *invest* with presents. New markets were rapidly opened up among middle-class youth and new sales territories were conquered in the suburbs, in rural areas, even in the colleges. We are in the presence of an enormous growth-industry, part of what *Forbes* has called the sybarition market.

High-consumption drug taking among the young has prepared the field for heroin. Even among the young subjected to cultural leveling, there are still cultural and class differences beneath the dreary uniformity of their clothes and talk; but these differences merely reflect stylistic differences in the reasons why one takes junk in the first place. What all have in common is that they have been intensively trained to need, to consume. All junkies are leveled and ultimately function in the same way. Middle-class youth has been drawn to marijuana, hashish, acid, mescaline, speed. Accompanying these usages was a mystique of community and the vast attempt to set up alternate political and economic entities. Having assumed that the technological millennium was here, the basic task was to create Eden on earth again. But they failed to understand their status as a dependent class and to deal with the contributory tensions of dependency: they also failed to understand the generalized hostility from a population with other cultural investments: they had transformed consuming *things* into consuming *experiences*, so while there was an indication for the withdrawal of luxury and leisure spending, the internalized pressures to consume and spend were not withdrawn. It was possibly this cognitive dissonance which was most unbearable. As in all millennial situations, the investment in ecstasy was heavy and ecstasy was drug-related, creating an ambience for the use of drugs in any direction; at the same time increments of toxicity stored in bodies created conditions of perpetual intoxication and lowered resistance to what formerly would have been recognized as dangerous. At the same time this population succeeded in making of itself a kind of *lumpen* proletariat, with *lumpen* omniverousness, a secondary labor force. When the years of highness had taken their toll, youth was ready, in great part, for the calming influences of barbiturates and heroin. And heroin, as we have pointed out, is a way of bringing these self-primitivized and tribal individuals back into the twentieth century. This proved easier than many anticipated, for while many thought that true communalism had been achieved and the twentieth century could be resisted from the inside, the fact was that the drugs, all drugs, masked what was in fact a greater alienation of person from person; they felt together but acted apart: a further breaking down of social relations.

Further, now that the traditional modes of training for role and class have weakened more and more, youth, as a general grouping without a set investment in ongoing society, tends to be rebellious and is the class most likely to revolt. It is at youth then, that the main thrust of the sales campaign has been aimed. *Junkies do not band together in associations and are therefore politically defused*; in the world of the junkie it is a war of all against all: total competition. And it is most necessary to start these work habits early: the ten-year-old junkie is in the cards.

In the past, drugs have worked to politically pacify the ghettos, training youth to the work ethic and providing the opportunity to erect a whole infrastructure of distributors, salesmen, and customers who have an ongoing investment and will themselves work to depoliticize, contain, coopt, or kill off those who threaten the market; for political militance leads to the nonconsumption of drugs in the long run, particularly heroin. We have only to remember the role played by heroin some years ago in breaking up the fighting gangs of New York City. If Jerry Rubin speaks of a whole generation of fifteen-year-old stoned terrorists, it is more meaningful to speak of a whole generation of fifteen-year-old stoned businessmen, providing the one area where the young, trained for little at this point, can be brought into intensive economic behavior by becoming pushers and junkies: where else can the unskilled make quick killings?

Are there drawbacks to the growth of an addicted population? What about the deaths?

To view the deaths of a few thousand children as alarming is to take the short-range view. The deaths are merely a function of the chaos of the market which is growing faster than it can be rationalized, leading to a woeful lack of standards in product preparation. A sort of industrial accident, if you will. In time regulation will solve this problem. The deaths have to be entered and written off as one of the social overheads of this New Economic Policy.

The junkie himself is a high consumer of what is, as William Burroughs has pointed out, the almost perfect commodity. The ideal nature of heroin lies in the fact that each dosage incorporates a built-in obsolescence and demands a constantly escalating consumption *linked to the conditions of illegality, deprivation, unregulated dosage.* While insecurity brought about by intense competition and constant danger creates an additional increment of tension, this tension can only be relieved by heightened dosages and is a spur to heightened consumption, tied to the need to evangelize new consumers who help to reinforce and stabilize, by mere numbers, the world of the junkie. In short, the heightened national tensions in a time of change determine the velocity of national addiction, and the social relations in the world of the junkie determine the intensity of addiction. The point is that mere legalization of smack cannot alleviate the problem at this stage, since the other need-relations of drug consumption, the mystiques, the rites, hipness, manhood, status, symbols of possession, sudden riches, guilt, legal insecurity and excitement, even romantic destruction of the self, the whole paraphernalia of addiction are not satisfied.

(Rich junkies do not have the same needs as poor junkies: there's a class content to addiction.)

The junkie is a veritable heroic Stakhanovite worker, almost pure economic man, living for the fix, the hunt, the fix, keeping his body alive merely to consume heroin at a rising rate, at the same time circulating enormous quantities of money, retaining only the modest interest of the fix which constantly diminishes (a sort of compound dis-interest) as his habit grows and the product continues to be adulterated. The actual heroin content of a bag is so low that it becomes obvious that it is the *whole pattern* of repetitive behavior, with the attendant feelings, that is most addictive, proving once again Nelson Algren's first law of addiction: we are all habituals. It is in the nature of a high-velocity, high-pressure business cycle that it demands total attention to that business alone. All previous relations that get in the way of the "getting and spending" cycle drop off: family loyalty, sexual feelings, love, cohort loyalty, friendship, brotherhood, compassion. The junkie will be driven to use any means necessary to get the money to buy the product. There's nothing like heroin consumption to teach the real meaning of the work ethic. It is on the junkie's back that a vast economic edifice is being built, one which resolves many economic and political difficulties.

For example, some of the spin-off industries called into being and supported by the junkie's work are:

Money-capital formation which takes a variety of paths before finding legitimate outlets, whether here or in some other country: the Mafia may bank in Switzerland, but what investments are in the Swiss bank's portfolio?

Additional nontaxed supplements are provided for police incomes, for the heroin industry is a semi-protected industry. This works in two ways: bribes, and money realized from police resale of confiscated heroin on the junkie market. This money doesn't stop on the police level but is further drawn upward, where it is distributed among district attorneys, judges, legislators, finds its way into political campaign chests.

Alarm over the spread of drug use leads to the beefing up of police forces all over the country and the potential growth of police forces as a separate political entity: crime rise used as a mode of getting allocation of funds for personnel and technology. At the same time there are the makings of a vast spy force in the form of undercover agents who may be used for other purposes. One example of the rationalization of drug-work linkages is the example of addicts as narcos, supporting their habits by this work, persuaded by the possibility of legal penalty as well as the threat of having their drug supply dried up. This force may be used to ensure tranquillity in a time of national retooling.

Sybarition spin-offs, such as the vast growing market in prostitution. This is particularly useful among the permanent female unemployables of the population for fighting off the threat of Women's Liberation.

Medical and drug company growth accompanies the use of heroin. Doctors come up with varieties of cure for the problem. Under the lash of competition, drug companies are led to allocate more and more resources to the production of competing drugs, such as barbiturates and amphetamines. The production of methadone, presumably useful in the combating of or substitution for heroin, has grown enormously; and methadone, as some junkies report, is a better high.

Millions have been invested in the purchase of sites, deteriorated, decayed, or deserted buildings for rehabilitation centers: architects and remodelers have been hired; phantom, but paid-for plans have been generated for centers that have not been built, and never will be. But then the newer capitalism does not require tangibles, but faith in process.

There is, of course, a fantastic rise in the therapy market. Theories of addiction cause and its cures proliferate. Studies are financed. Pilot programs are funded. New jargons develop. Again, each psychosocial theory of the cause and cure of the habit doesn't have to be valid: what is valid is the ability to sell the theory, to get funding for the theory, to convince some legislator (and possibly addicts) that the program works, to demonstrate some successes, and to generate in the wake of failures still further programs. Social scientists compete fiercely on the open program market for funding, and competition is the spur to the growth of a body of scientific capital: the point is to get that program on the market first and sell it. This has also given rise to a new job category: the professional junkie who goes from program to program getting funds to keep alive, demonstrating the success of each program. There are those who carp that these theories are, in fact, forms of Lysenkoist science, rigged cure-counts and all. This is to take a noneconomic view of things. Admittedly there are no cures, nor has the *problem* been approached from the right angle, nor does anyone, to date, seem to know much about the total syndrome of addiction, but this is to assume that one considers heroin addiction a problem and not a way of generating enterprise and capital. In its wake a large apparatus of social workers, counselors, reformed-junkie lecturers, psychiatrists, writers of books and articles, psychologists, political, administrative, and clerical jobs is created, as well as a mode of job retraining for a whole body of social and poverty workers whose situation is threatened by massive cutbacks in the poverty programs. More:

being in key positions to see economic possibilities, many of these people break their bureaucratic/professional relations and enter the market as pushers and middlemen.

Most of the therapy rites in addict cure have taken their lead from the techniques evolved by Alcoholics Anonymous, a variant of Christian Redemption, built around the concept that addiction reflects certain inherent psychological instabilities and character deformations. The pattern is familiar: the weakness, the temptations, the self-indulgence, the rise and fall and the redemption through recognition and perception of oneself as a child of original sin. To be sure these weaknesses are spoken of in psychological rather than in traditional Christian terms, but the whole Christian journey of self-degradation, self-negation, the trip through hell, the public confession, the self-abasement, the blinding insight, the revival, and the salvation is evoked. The aim is to reintroduce the *need*, if not to abstain, to at least self-regulate one's hungers, to introduce planning and long-range goals into the pursuit of instant gratification, and finally redeem one to the Protestant Ethic. This becomes a drama which is acted out again and again and can usually be sustained with the use of methadone.

Ingenious black-market activities have sprung up: for instance, *clean* urine is sold to users who have to report to probation officers.

Of course the most lucrative spin-off industry has been stealing, which has the feature of being able to loosen vast quantities of capital frozen in already purchased artifacts. An estimate of the amounts of material stolen is staggering. Roughly speaking, stolen goods are resold at anywhere from one-fifth to one-hundredth of the original value, depending, of course, on the condition of the goods and the pressing needs of the junkie (we have heard of a new IBM Selectric typewriter sold for $20). This leads to the replacement of stolen items through personal spending, tax write-offs, insurance, which in turn stimulates the consumption market. Even factories deal heavily in the purchase of stolen goods. We are talking about something like a thirty-billion-dollar-a-year turnover. This has provided for a new mode of distributing wealth without resorting to socialist or communist methods, retaining free enterprise.

The rise in the home-security market is stunning. Alarm systems, unbreakable locks and grates and chains are devised; dogs are bought; weaponry is purchased. Old forms of free association are revived; vigilante groupings and paramilitary police forces spring up once more.

In short, the growth possibilities are exhilarating. It would take one of Wassily Leontief's input-output charts to chronicle the basic implications of this infra-economy.

It will ultimately be necessary to rationalize the market. This should be done in two ways. In the ghettos, heroin consumption should be permitted to rise among the unemployables, continuing the depoliticizing effect and fostering free enterprise and competition in a free market. As far as the potential work force is concerned, it will be necessary to find a chemical and artificially produced substitute for heroin, such as methadone, with a constant dosage made readily available to addicts, tied into an extensive Christianizing/therapy work program which will make for a tractable labor force: at specific times in the day one could have a break for getting stoned rather than a coffee break. Work loads could be met with the proper drugs: speed for speedups, downs for slack times. Already there is evidence that small ghetto employers give their workers fix money at lunch time. Further, artificial drugs could be made at home and thus reduce the disadvantage of America in the international balance of payments, and wouldn't be dependent on the vagaries of nature for production. If this market could be regulated, then we can avoid the mistakes of the prerevolutionary Chinese. And in time, to stand F. Scott Fitzgerald on his head, the orgiastic future will no longer recede from us.

Appendix

THE WORLD HEROIN PROBLEM

Introduction

Drug abuse around the world is increasing. Of particular concern is the alarming rise in the use of opium-based drugs, particularly heroin, in the United States, and the rapid increase in heroin addiction within the United States military forces in South Vietnam, where the best estimates are that as many as 10 to 15 percent of our servicemen are addicted to heroin in one form or another.

To combat this growing menace around the world and at home the United States must use every resource available. It must work through international organizations; it must exert pressure on its friends and allies to convince them of the need to take strong action either to control or to eliminate the growing of opium poppies or to increase their efforts to stop the illegal traffic in narcotics. Our nation must provide the leadership to make international cooperation to control the illegal traffic in narcotics and other dangerous drugs more effective.

The battle to stem the alarming increase in heroin addiction will not be easy, nor will victory come quickly. But the war against heroin must be sharply accelerated —now. Given the increasing use of heroin among our youth, immediate action is crucial. Unfortunately, time is not on our side, and as this report is being written more young Americans are becoming addicted to heroin.

Equally distressing is the fact that the United States alone cannot bring an end to the waste and devastation that drug abuse, particularly the use of opium and its derivatives, is causing among the youth of the nation. We must have the cooperation of the entire world.

For example, only a small percentage of the illegal heroin that reaches the United States is confiscated by the authorities. There are simply too many ways of hiding heroin, from small containers secreted in various body orifices to hollow ski poles and food containers. There are literally thousands of places to hide illegal heroin on board ships entering U.S. ports. International air travel has complicated the problem even further, for it enables the courier or trafficker to move quickly from continent to continent, arranging pickups and payoffs personally, in addition to providing places to secrete illegal shipments.

Once the poppy pod is cut and the opium gum extracted and sold on the illegal market, the battle to prevent the end product, heroin, from reaching the addict is lost. The problem must be attacked at the source—in the poppy fields of the Near and Far East, principally in Turkey, Thailand, Burma, and Laos.

We must be willing to devote more resources, human and material, to fight the illegal international traffic in heroin, including the exercise of economic and political pressures where necessary. If that means the imposition of economic sanctions or the exercise of political initiatives, we must be willing to follow that course of action. We are fighting to save generations of young Americans from the scourge of heroin. As in any war, we must bring all of the weapons available to the point of decision.

The Heroin Problem in the United States

THE PROBLEM OF HEROIN ADDICTION IN THE UNITED STATES

The National Institute of Mental Health estimates that there are 250,000 heroin addicts in the United States. One half of these are located in the New York City area.

In 1970, 1,154 persons died as a result of drug addiction in the nation's largest city. One half of these deaths occurred among young people twenty-three years of age, or less.

In a 1970 survey in the District of Columbia, heroin addiction was estimated at 10,400 persons. In 1971, this estimate had risen to 16,880, an increase of more than 60 percent.

There are approximately 9,000 heroin addicts in Chicago, according to the narcotics squad of that city.

Heroin addiction among U.S. military forces has reached alarming proportions. Reliable authorities estimate that as many as 10 to 15 percent of the troops in Vietnam are using heroin in one form or another. Some smoke it, some sniff or "snort," and approximately 5 to 10 percent inject.

Five years ago the heroin problem was restricted to the ghetto areas of our major cities. Now it is spreading to the suburbs and is found among the children of the wealthy and well-to-do as well as among the poor.

The heroin problem is also affecting U.S. industry. The *Wall Street Journal*, quoting from a study conducted by the New York Chamber of Commerce, reported last summer that "drug abuse in business—a problem which was rare, indeed, two years ago has overnight become—in qualitative terms—almost as serious as that of alcoholism."

"The increase in drug abuse on company premises stems partly from the spread of illegal drugs through high schools and college campuses and U.S. troops in Vietnam," the report concluded.

And the number of addicts is increasing rapidly. In a statement to the United Nations Commission on Narcotics at Geneva in September 1970, John E. Ingersoll, director of the Bureau of Narcotics and Dangerous Drugs (BNDD), said that "the list of addicts is growing by several thousand each year and, in 1969, the number of new addicts doubled from the preceding year. Every time one addict is cured, more take his place because of the ever-increasing amounts of heroin available. Among the other debilitating consequences of the addiction problem is that in New York City alone, persons are dying of drug related causes at the rate of three per day."

Even these statistics, alarming as they are, may not tell the whole story. Unfortunately, the extent of the addiction problem is difficult to measure. There is no central agency in the United States which collects all of the intelligence on the number of drugs users, and the figures provided by BNDD are minimal estimates, since they are based only on reporting from law enforcement agencies.

The statistics that are available, therefore, are only educated guesses, and the number of addicts may be greatly in excess of the estimated 250,000.

CONSUMPTION OF HEROIN IN THE UNITED STATES

Based on the estimates that there are at least 250,000 heroin addicts in the United States, it would take between four and five tons of heroin to support the addict population.

Estimates of the cost of the heroin that the average addict requires daily vary, however, from $30 to $100 per day.

HEROIN ADDICTION AND CRIME IN THE UNITED STATES

The habit of the narcotics addict is not only a danger to himself, but to society as a whole. Narcotics have been cited as a primary cause of the enormous increase in crimes committed over the past few years.

Whatever the price, the cost in property stolen by the addict to support the habit is tremendous.

The estimated amount of money spent by heroin addicts in the United States is $7.5 million per day. This figure is based on the fact that there are 250,000 addicts, with an average habit (minimum) of $30 daily. For this year [1971], the estimated figure would be approximately $2,737,500,000.

To support the habit, reliable authorities estimate that the addict would have to steal goods worth at least four or five times the cost of his habit per year.

If 75 percent of those addicted resorted to crime, using the above figures, then, the cost in crime committed to sustain the habit would be in excess of $8 billion per year at a minimum.

THE SOURCE OF ILLICIT HEROIN

Most world poppy cultivation takes place within a zone extending from the plains of Anatolia in Turkey to Yünnan province in China. The international illegal traffic in opium has two major production areas. The first area of importance for the United States is in the Near East, where opium produced in Turkey for legitimate medical requirements is diverted to illegal channels. The opium is smuggled to Syria and Lebanon, where it is processed into morphine base. (A certain amount of morphine base and heroin is also produced in Turkey.) The morphine base is then smuggled to the Marseilles area of France, where it is refined into heroin in clandestine laboratories. The bulk of the heroin entering the United States is grown in Turkey and processed in Marseilles.

The second important area is in the Far East, particularly in Laos, Burma, and Thailand, and to a lesser degree, Yünnan province in China.

At least 1,000 tons of raw opium are produced in the Shan states of Burma, the border area of Yünnan province in China, northern Thailand, and northwestern Laos, and Burma meet. A large proportion of the where there is little or no governmental control by either Burma, Laos, or Thailand.

The central collecting point for the majority of this opium is at a point where the borders of Thailand, Laos, and Burma meet. A large proportion of the opium is designated for Southeast Asian opium addicts. The remainder either is exported outside of Southeast Asia or is refined into morphine base, the basic ingredient of heroin, or heroin itself in laboratories located in the Burmese-Laotian-Thailand border area, in Vientiane, Laos, in Bangkok, Thailand, and at other points along the Mekong. The heroin labs manufacture both No. 3 purple smoking heroin, which is used by Asian addicts, and No. 4 white heroin, which is produced primarily for the U.S. market and for U.S. troops in South Vietnam.

The main flow of No. 4 heroin to U.S. troops in South Vietnam is through Laos and Thailand. In addition, large quantities of opium and morphine base are smuggled into Hong Kong, where it is both consumed locally and refined into No. 4 heroin for the U.S. market.[1] U.S. narcotics experts regard Hong Kong of increasing importance as a source of the heroin being smuggled to the United States from the Far East. Current estimates are that at least 10 percent of the heroin entering the United States comes from the Far East and that the percentage is growing. There is also evidence that some of the No. 4 heroin appearing in Saigon also has its source in Hong Kong.

A Chinese traveler from Hong Kong was arrested at Tan Son Nhut in April 1971 carrying three and one-

[1] Opium and morphine base are smuggled into Hong Kong primarily in Thai fishing boats. It is processed into heroin in four or five clandestine laboratories. The authorities in Hong Kong have a difficult time intercepting shipments from Thailand. The Thai fishing boats dump the opium into Chinese Communist waters where it is picked up by one of the 11,000 junks that ply the waters around Hong Kong. The job of policing and seizing is almost impossible. As in the case of Turkey, once the poppy is cut and the opium introduced into illegal channels, the battle to prevent the end product from falling into the hands of the addict is lost.

half kilos of heroin. This could be the beginning of a trend. When the heroin dealers in Hong Kong realize that a lucrative market exists among the Americans in South Vietnam, they will undoubtedly attempt to get into the market.

There has recently been an increase in the amount of No. 4 heroin smuggled directly from Thailand to the United States. Narcotics experts attribute the increase primarily to the expanding activity of a number of ex-servicemen and U.S. nationals who have served in Southeast Asia and have set up smuggling operations in Thailand.

A certain amount of heroin is also produced from opium poppies grown in Mexico. It is estimated that Mexico accounts for about 15 percent of the heroin which is smuggled into the United States. There is no evidence available to suggest that the Chinese Communists are actively engaged in the illegal international traffic in opium or its derivatives.

PROFITS FROM THE PRODUCTION, PROCESSING, AND SALE OF ILLEGAL OPIUM

One of the fundamental facts mitigating against solution of the heroin problem both in the United States and abroad is the tremendous profit involved. From the prices paid to the poppy grower to the retail price for pure heroin sold in New York, there is a $219,975 markup as shown in the following table:

Because of the tremendous profits that are realized as a result of the illegal traffic in narcotics, there is always the possibility that governmental authorities and police

Development of Retail Price of Heroin in the United States, 1969

United States	U.S. dollars per kilogram	U.S. dollars per kilogram of raw opium equivalent
Price to farmer for opium (in Turkey)	$25	
Wholesale price for heroin* (Marseilles)	5,000	$500
Border price for heroin (New York)	10,000	1,000
Wholesale price for heroin (New York)	22,000	2,200
Retail price for heroin (New York)	220,000	22,000

* When raw opium is converted to morphine and heroin the volume is reduced by a ratio of 10 to 1.

at all levels "can be bought." Above all, some way must be found to take the profit out of heroin smuggling.

The Situation in France and Italy

FRANCE

HEROIN PRODUCTION IN FRANCE

Heroin is produced in illegal laboratories primarily in the Marseilles area, although some may also be produced in Paris and Le Havre. The principal area is Marseilles because of the port facilities and the large criminal element located there. Marseilles is also closer to the source of supply, Turkey, than either Paris or Le Havre, although there is evidence that increasing amounts of morphine base are being smuggled into West Germany by Turkish nationals employed in that country. If this trend continues, other areas of Europe could be used to produce heroin. This will be particularly true if current efforts to close down the illicit laboratories in Marseilles prove successful.

It has been estimated that 80 percent of the heroin entering the United States originates in Turkish poppy fields and is processed in France. French authorities question this estimate. From the discussion which the study group has had with authorities in France, Turkey, and the United States, this estimate is undoubtedly high. It is fair to say, however, that the bulk of the heroin entering the United States does originate in Turkish poppy fields and is processed in France. According to the experts, French heroin is among the best grade made, owing to the expertise of the French chemists who process the morphine into heroin. By the time it reaches the addict in the United States, it has been reduced to 4 to 6 percent purity.

THE MARSEILLES HEROIN OPERATION

Most of the illegal heroin-producing laboratories are located on the southern coast of France, between Nice and Marseilles, and possibly in Corsica.

These laboratories are not large, and a number are believed to be mobile. They do not operate continuously, as it does not take long to process a shipment of morphine base into heroin. According to the best estimates, there are probably only five to ten laboratories operating at any one time.

The poppy is grown in Turkey and the opium smuggled to Marseilles by sea, air, and overland. Once it arrives in Marseilles it is picked up by the purchaser and turned over to a chemist for processing.

The chemist usually operates his own laboratory, frequently on a free-lance basis. There is no one central organization commanding the entire operation, although cooperation among groups is not unusual. If a shipment to one group is seized by the police, another group will help by loaning it some morphine base to tide the losing group over until it can arrange for another shipment from Turkey.

It is estimated that there are five and possibly ten, groups operating at any one time with up to 100 individuals employed. Each group appears to have its own courier and trafficking and purchasing operations. Over the past ten years every narcotics case in Marseilles has involved one or more of four Corsican families: the Venturi brothers (Jean and Dominic), Marcel Francisci, Antoine Guerini, and Joseph Orsini. (Orsini himself served a prison term in the United States and was deported in 1958.) There are offshoots of these four families and ad hoc groups may appear from time to time, but these four families are the heart of illegal heroin production in Marseilles. The problem is that in France, as well as in the United States, the police must have evidence upon which to base a case. The police cannot put the finger on the families or people involved. French authorities are hampered by the secret Swiss bank accounts as much as are U.S. authorities.

FRENCH MECHANISMS FOR CONTROL

Though France does not suffer to the same extent from heroin abuse as the United States, there is a problem developing in that country. This has been a major factor in prompting French authorities to increase their efforts to combat the availability of heroin in France. An indispensable element in this endeavor has been a growing willingness to cooperate with the United States in its efforts to fight heroin abuse.

A French-American agreement setting up close cooperation between the agencies specializing in the fight against the illegal traffic in drugs in France and the United States was signed on February 26, 1971, by Raymond Marcellin, French Minister of the Interior, and U.S. Attorney General John M. Mitchell. Under the terms of the agreement both governments have agreed to exchange narcotics agents in order to facilitate cooperation. Very considerable credit belongs to Mr. Marcellin for assigning high priority to the anti-heroin effort.

The fight against drug abuse in France is centralized in the Office of the Chief of National Narcotics and Dangerous Drugs Bureau.

There are three groups which deal with narcotics matters: the Central Office, the Marseilles Service, and the Narcotics Service in Paris.

In 1969 there were 40 agents assigned to narcotics duties; in 1971 there were 120 with the probability that this number would be increased shortly.

In addition, between 6,000 and 7,000 police and gendarmerie and others have been given training in narcotics control practices.

It was pointed out that under the centralized French system, numbers were not as important as emphasis.

If any information becomes available to any French authority, it will be transmitted to the central office, although at the present time French authorities are working largely from information provided by the United States.

The French authorities believe that the effort against drug traffickers must be secret. In their opinion the nature of the problem is such that the less known about police methods and tactics, the better the chances are for successful results. As a result, police throughout the country sometimes work on narcotics cases without being completely aware of all the facts surrounding the case. This approach also serves to prevent police corruption.

French police do very little undercover work. Under French law even police officials are not permitted to get involved in narcotics traffic. If they do, they are liable to criminal prosecution. In addition, if it could be shown that the evidence was provoked by police activity the case would be thrown out of court. As a consequence, the French police depend upon U.S. personnel for their information.

DIFFICULTIES IN CONTROLLING ILLEGAL HEROIN PRODUCTION IN FRANCE

The French police have been able to locate and close only 13 laboratories over the past 20 years. Two were closed in 1969; one in 1964. One of those closed in 1969 was located in a villa approximately 25 kilometers outside of Marseilles. Finding this one was a result of fine police work by both the French police and United States BNDD agents working closely with the police. A man suspected of being implicated in the narcotics racket was released from arrest. He went directly to the villa and was followed by the authorities. When the police raided the villa, the laboratory was in full operation.

The study mission inspected another building in the suburbs of Marseilles which had housed the illicit laboratory that was closed in 1964. It was an innocent-looking building, and if the authorities had not been told by an informer that a laboratory was located in that particular building it would not have been discovered.

As a result of visiting these two locations, it became evident to us that looking for an illegal heroin-producing laboratory is like looking for a needle in a haystack. They can be set up anywhere in a short period of time and they can be moved just as quickly.

At present, the only practical method by which they can be located is through the use of informers. This takes time and money. Money must also be available to pay the informer as well as for making a purchase of the heroin from illegal sources in order to develop leads.

Both French and American authorities voiced confidence that their efforts were progressing satisfactorily and that the Marseilles Service and the central office were developing a force capable of effective action in discovering and closing the illegal laboratories. There is a steadily increasing spirit of aggressiveness on the part of the French authorities in their efforts to stop the illegal production of heroin in France.

The French authorities were also hopeful that scientific and technological developments would greatly assist them in their investigations. For example, now in the process of development is a sensory device which, when perfected, will "smell" illegal laboratories in operation. These devices will be mounted in helicopters which will be used by the police to patrol the area. Unfortunately, the device must be in an area when a laboratory is in operation if it is to be useful to the police.

Helicopter-borne patrols are of considerable assistance to the police and should be used. If nothing else, they can increase the sense of police pressure that the narcotics manufacturer is beginning to feel in France. The authorities were emphatic in their belief that, because of French narcotics laws and police pressure, the laboratory operators are beginning to "panic." Police pressure, should, therefore, be increased.

Consideration should be given to making helicopters and trained pilots available to the French until they develop their own capabilities. If arrangements can be made with French governmental officials it might be possible to place U.S. helicopter units assigned to U.S. forces in Europe on temporary duty in the Marseilles area. While this would be only an interim solution to the problem, it would be useful and it would enable the authorities to utilize one more weapon in the struggle to stamp out illicit heroin production during the period when the French are developing their own airborne patrol capability.

ITALY

Italy is a transshipment point. It is estimated that 30 to 40 percent of the raw material used to produce heroin either passes through Italy or is hidden in vessels destined for France which stop at Italian ports.

There is also the probability that some of the heroin produced in France and elsewhere returns to Italy, where it is then smuggled to the United States. There are no firm estimates on the amount involved, but it is considered to be substantial by knowledgeable experts. The number of known heroin traffickers seen in Italy plus the deep involvement of a number of known Mafiosa in the United States form the basis for this judgment.

There is also the possibility that heroin is being produced in Sicily and Sardinia.

ITALIAN EFFORTS TO CONTROL THE ILLEGAL TRAFFIC IN NARCOTICS

Efforts by the Italian government to control the illegal traffic in narcotics have not been successful. For example, it is estimated that the Italian authorities seize only about one tenth of 1 percent of the narcotics which reach that country.

There appear to be a number of reasons for this.

First, the Italian police agencies are fragmented, and cooperation depends upon personalities rather than institutional procedures. There are three distinct national police agencies: the Finance Police, the Public Security Forces, and the Carabinieri. Each is jealous of its prerogatives.

In addition, a Central Narcotics Office (CNO) has been set up in the Ministry of the Interior. Charged with the responsibility for coordinating efforts to control narcotics traffic, the CNO does not always get the cooperation of the police agencies or high-ranking government officials.

Second, the Mafia is deeply involved in the narcotics traffic, and high-ranking Italian government officials aid that organization throughout Europe. A commission has been appointed to determine the extent of Mafia infiltration of the Italian government. It will take some time, however, before the results of this study are known.

Third, the Italians do not recognize the seriousness of this problem. According to police authorities throughout Italy, there is no Italian heroin problem. Consequently, there is no feeling of urgency to take immediate and effective action to coordinate their efforts to combat this problem.

Fourth, the Italians will not take action to improve international cooperation to stop the illegal traffic of heroin. They do not coordinate their activities with the International Criminal Police Organization (Interpol) in spite of the fact that that organization maintains complete files on all known international criminals. Nor will they pass information to Interpol. They have also refused to put any pressure on Turkey to do anything about this problem. Another indication of Italian attitudes is their refusal to participate in the Special Drug Abuse Control Fund established by the United Nations until at least three fourths of the members have contributed.

ITALIAN COOPERATION WITH THE UNITED STATES

There are BNDD agents in Italy working with the Italian authorities in an effort to interdict morphine passing through Italy and to stop heroin from returning. These efforts are hampered by the need to coordinate activities within the several Italian police agencies. Nevertheless, BNDD is helping and encouraging the Italians to improve their capability to halt the drug traffic while waiting for the Italian government to centralize its operations in this area. Right now, there is little or no cooperation between the Central Narcotics Office and the several police agencies, including the local police. As a matter of fact, the only successful seizures and arrests made in Italy since 1962 have been made with BNDD assistance.

Ambassador Graham Martin has met with Italian government officials on at least three occasions requesting more cooperation from the Italian government, to no avail.

These efforts must be intensified. The United States must keep the pressure on the government of Italy to take effective action and should be prepared, if necessary, to supply aircraft, helicopters, vehicles, communication and other equipment to help increase Italian capabilities to deal effectively with the illegal traffic in narcotics.

If there were no opium production in Turkey, however, the illegal laboratories in Marseilles could not exist. Nor could the illegal trafficker profit in Italy. Solution to the problem has to be found in Turkey. If efforts to close the illegal laboratories in Marseilles or to stop the Italian trafficker are successful, the operation will move some place else. Without morphine base it is impossible to produce heroin. The Middle East-European aspect of the illegal international traffic in narcotics can be stopped only at the source—in the poppy fields of Turkey.

The Role of Turkey

BACKGROUND

Poppy cultivation is a tradition in the Anatolian region of Turkey dating back to about 1900 B.C. During the nineteenth century, as world trade greatly expanded, the demand for opium increased, and between 1850 and 1900 cultivation spread and expanded throughout the entire country as a cash crop and an important export. In addition to opium gum, other important by-products include seeds for flavoring and oil, both of which have become a standard part of the Turkish farmer's diet.

Although by 1900 the addiction and abuse of opium and its derivatives had become a serious world health problem and the need for controls was recognized, the political, cultural, social, and economic differences between nations made achivement possible only through a progression of treaties, culminating finally in their codification in a Single Convention in 1961. The Single Narcotics Convention which came into force in 1964 was ratified by Turkey in December 1966 and by the United States in 1967. Under this agreement Turkey is recognized as an opium exporter to the legal market.

ATTEMPTS TO CONTROL OPIUM PRODUCTION

Since 1967 Turkey has reduced the number of provinces legally permitted to cultivate poppies from 21 to 7 for the 1971 harvest. It has announced a further reduction to 4 provinces for 1972. During this same period the legal production of opium gum has been reduced from 368 tons to an estimated 100 tons in 1970. It is estimated by reliable authorities, however, that illegal production could be at least as much and possibly twice that amount—more than enough to satisfy the 4 to 5 tons of heroin required by the addict population in the United States.

Turkey has also tightened procedures for surveillance of poppy fields, purchase from farmers, and curbing of illegal traffic, and instituted efforts to encourage crop substitutions.

Under current practice, world-wide opium trade requirements are determined by the United Nations Control Board. Based upon this, the Turkish government estimates how much opium Turkey should produce in the following year. The Ministry of Agriculture then determines how much acreage should be planted and in which provinces. The cabinet then passes an approving decree. The Ministry does not tell the farmer how much land he can plant. Instead, the farmer declares to the village headman how much he intends to farm and the expected yield. These estimates are then passed to the Ministry of Agriculture. The farmer is expected to abide by his declaration, but under present law he is not required to obtain a license.

Control teams will be organized in each of the four provinces to monitor the growing of poppies. These teams will inspect the fields continually from the time of planting through the harvest. The control team will also be responsible for inspecting those areas where poppy cultivation is not permitted. To ensure that the provincial control teams are managing the program properly, other inspection teams will be periodically sent from Ankara. To facilitate the inspection process the United States will probably loan an airplane to the Turkish Marketing Organization (TMO) to help in the surveillance. The control teams will also educate the farmer on the reasons and the need to eradicate poppy growing in Turkey.

The government of Turkey has also increased its efforts to purchase the total opium crop being produced this year. Special instructions have been given to the TMO, which is the agency responsible for all purchases and sales of opium. In addition, the governors of the provinces currently harvesting opium have been instructed to assure the closest cooperation among TMO, Ministry of Agriculture, and law enforcement agencies in their provinces.

The basic problem in any collection system is to get an accurate measure of how much is actually planted and how much opium gum is produced. If the above system is effective, the illegal production of opium should be reduced. These procedures are not, however, a substitute for a licensing law. Under this procedure the only penalty is to deny the farmer the authorization to grow poppies. These steps, however, do represent an effort to bring poppy cultivation under control.

Hopefully, once poppy cultivation is brought under control, the next step should be a decision to stop growing poppies entirely. To do this, the farmer must be taught to grow other crops. This should not be an insurmountable problem. Poppy cultivation represents only a minor portion of the crop land. The poppy grower seldom devotes more than one hectare to poppies. The poppy takes so much out of the soil that there is a need to rotate crops. If modern farming methods could be introduced and crops that are easier on the soil developed, the incentive to grow poppies might be removed.

To encourage crop substitution, the Ministry of Agriculture has appointed at least one extension agent to each county in the poppy cultivation area. Depending upon soil and climatic conditions, farmers are being encouraged and assisted to switch to other cash crops, including fruits and vegetables, safflower, sunflower, alfalfa, vetch, and wheat. A new high-yielding winter wheat seed has been introduced on the Anatolia Plateau, which includes some of the poppy-growing provinces.

The matter of crop substitution is a long-term problem. The government of Turkey has yet to develop any particular crop that would pay the farmer the same amount of income as that derived from the legal and illegal production of opium. While there are crops that would pay the farmer the same amount of money that he now derives from the legal cultivation of poppies, there is no other crop which would equal the total income from both legal and illegal production.

In an effort to induce the Turkish farmer to grow other crops, consideration should be given to discontinuing poppies as a cash crop. It is one of two crops grown in Turkey for which payment by the government is immediate. The other is sugar beets.

If the government were to increase the payments for sugar beets and encourage the substitution of wheat or some other crop for the poppy as a cash crop, the results might be encouraging. If necessary, the United States should help in this effort by vigorously pressing the Turkish government to consider this alternative and by furnishing financial and technical assistance to implement such a program.

Consideration should also be given to the feasibility of increasing the price that the government pays the farmer for opium gum. This action, combined with strict licensing laws and other measures which would make possession of, and trafficking in, illegal opium or its derivatives a crime punishable by death, as in Iran, could produce positive results.

ECONOMIC FACTORS INVOLVED IN TURKISH POPPY GROWING

If Turkey stopped growing poppies completely there would be slight impact upon the Turkish economy. According to official Turkish government statistics, Turkey's total export earnings in 1969 were 4.8 billion Turkish lira (TL) or approximately $534 million, at the rate of 9 lira to the dollar. Legal exports of opium products—opium gum and poppy straw—in that year were valued at only TL 23.6 million or $2,622,196.

Illegal sales of opium do not show up in these figures. If illegal opium sales netted the Turkish farmer even three times that amount or $7,866,588 this is an insignificant item in a total export earning of approximately $534 million.

There are now approximately 80,000 farmers engaged in growing poppies for opium production. In the late 1960's the average annual earnings per farm was between $700 and $800. Ten percent of this was derived from the sale, legal and illegal, of opium gum. This represents approximately one half of the total annual cash income of the Turkish farmer. The government pays between $10 and $15 per kilogram for legal opium. On the other hand, the farmer can sell opium on the illegal market for at least $25 per kilogram. Thus, the incentive is to sell to the illegal purchaser.

There is another problem. At present the farmer takes the opium gum to the government collector in his area, who is supposed to weigh the gum and pay the farmer on the spot.

In practice, the farmer is very often cheated. The TMO representative responsible for the purchase of the opium gum from the farmer frequently waits six weeks before he weighs the opium gum. During this time moisture in the gum has evaporated and the weight reduced. As a consequence, the farmer gets less money and he feels cheated. Under the circumstances it is no wonder that the farmer is more interested in selling on the black market.

WHAT TURKEY HAS NOT DONE

In 1966 Turkey ratified the Single Convention on Narcotic Drugs. Article 23 of the Convention requires that all parties enact licensing laws to control the growing of poppies. To date, Turkey has not passed a licensing law.

The principal reasons given are that domestic political realities (approximately 80,000 farmers grow poppies) do not permit passage, and that passage as a result of U.S. pressure would give the impression that the government of Turkey is a "puppet of the United States."

The Committee on Foreign Affairs has been studying this problem since July 1970. At that time passage of the licensing laws was thought imminent, before the

Turkish Parliament adjourned during the first week in August. No action was taken.

At the Geneva meeting of the United Nations Commission on Narcotics in September 1970 the Turkish representatives pledged passage of a licensing law shortly after Parliament convened early in November.

It is now May 1971 and no positive action has yet been taken by the Turkish Parliament. In response to questions by members of the study mission, a high-ranking Turkish official expressed strong belief that a licensing law would be passed this year.

The Demirel cabinet fell in March 1971, and a new cabinet has been installed under the leadership of Prime Minister Nihat Erim. This government is a nonparty government and is more broadly based than was the Demirel government. If it had the will to do so, it could pass quickly a law licensing the growing of poppies.

And while there are indications that the prime minister intends to take action to control the growing of poppies, the study mission is of the opinion that there is no sense of immediacy on the part of the Turkish government.

An extract from the Erim government's program fully illustrates this. "Our government is of the opinion that opium smuggling, which has become a destructive disaster of the youth of the world, is hurting above all our humane feelings; therefore, due importance shall be attached to this problem. Opium producers shall be provided with a better field of occupation in farming."

Certain Turkish legislators questioned the inclusion in the program of remarks on opium. The full response of Prime Minister Erim is not available; however, observers present report that he took a strong position in favor of opium production controls and then explained that opium production would not be discontinued completely until the farmers engaged in poppy farming and opium production were provided with means of attaining a higher level of subsistence.

While it is reassuring to learn that the government of Turkey is aware of the problem, it is well to remember that actions speak louder than words.

If the United States is to solve the problem of heroin addiction at home, it must have the active and effective cooperation of the Turkish government, for only the Turks have the power and the authority to control the growing of poppies. And while the United States can't tell the Turks what to do in this matter, it must employ every available leverage to persuade the Turkish government to take whatever steps are necessary to control and eventually discontinue the growing of poppies.

As a measure of Turkish sincerity in acting on this problem, it is essential that legislation controlling the growing of poppies be enacted as a meaningful first step. While passage of a licensing law will not solve the problem, it is required if the government of Turkey is to inhibit the flow of opium to the illegal market. Passage of this legislation would also demonstrate Turkey's desire to fulfill her treaty commitments under the provisions of the Single Convention—commitments that were made in December 1966.

UNITED STATES-TURKISH COOPERATION

In September 1966 the United States began discussions with the government of Turkey to find ways to better control the production of opium in Turkey. At that time poppy cultivation was permitted in 21 provinces. Although production was prohibited throughout the rest of Turkey, enforcement agencies were poorly equipped and relatively untrained for this type of control, resulting in an estimated 200 tons available for the illegal market.

By 1967, as a result of U.S. efforts and decreasing world opium requirements, the government of Turkey concluded that opium production would not be an economic crop in the future and that steps should be taken to reduce production. At the same time, the government decided that it needed to upgrade its enforcement capabilities as well as to provide assistance to farmers to switch to other crops.

To assist in this effort, in 1968 the United States made $3 million available from AID funds. Approximately $1.5 million of the loan is being used to finance vehicles and equipment for enforcement agencies and the remainder to finance research to develop alternative crops and vehicles and equipment required by the Ministry of Agriculture to assist the farmer in switching to other crops.

All of the commodities programmed under this loan have not been received in Turkey. Bureaucracy and red tape have held up the clearing of the commodities through Turkish customs, with the result that much of the equipment sits around on the dock for substantial periods of time. Steps are now being taken to ensure that equipment and commodities shipped for the use of the national police and gendarmerie will not be subjected to customs clearance.

In connection with this loan, the government of Turkey has reorganized the Turkish National Police and the gendarmerie in order to develop a 750-man narcotic law enforcement group. The headquarters of this group is located in Ankara, and when fully developed, it is expected that there will be 51 regional offices. At the present time it is estimated that half of the 750-man group has been trained and deployed in the field.

Cooperation between the U.S. Bureau of Narcotics and Dangerous Drugs and Turkish enforcement agencies has been excellent. BNDD agents are now in Turkey working with their counterparts on narcotics control. U.S. agents have reported little evidence of illicit production in provinces where poppy cultivation has been prohibited, and such crops, when found, have been immediately destroyed.

There have been suggestions that the United States make money available to Turkey to buy up the entire poppy crop. They have been rejected on the grounds that it would result in every farmer increasing the land that he devotes to poppy cultivation.

The suggestion has also been rejected by the Turkish government on the grounds that the domestic political situation in Turkey made it impossible. If this obstacle could be overcome, it is estimated that it would cost about $5 million to buy up the entire crop.

Another proposal worthy of consideration has been made that the U.S. attempt to purchase the entire illegal crop through the use of undercover agents. This would have the effect of drying up the source of morphine for the laboratories in Marseilles and if entirely successful would dry up the heroin supply to the U.S. market, at least temporarily. Consideration might be given to this expedient as a stopgap measure while other programs, such as crop substitution, are being developed.

It was also suggested to the study mission by a leading Turkish parliamentarian that a parliamentary group be established between the Congress of the United States and the Turkish Parliament for the purpose of discussing mutual problems in the field of narcotics control. In the opinion of the study mission such a group would be beneficial and would provide a useful forum for a meaningful exchange of views on the subject. It should not, however, become merely a discussion panel.

It has been argued that if the supply of opium from Turkey is shut off completely, those engaged in the illegal production of heroin would transfer their operations someplace else, possibly to Afghanistan, India, Iran, Thailand, etc.

There are valid arguments against this line of reasoning. In the first place, the heroin obtained from poppies grown in Afghanistan is low quality and cannot be produced in the quantities needed by the international heroin dealer. Second, most of the opium grown in Afghanistan is consumed either in Afghanistan or in Iran.

Iran has strict licensing laws and efficient collection procedures, and most of what she produces is also consumed domestically.

India also has strict licensing laws and efficient collection procedures. There is little evidence of a leakage of opium gum to the illicit market from India.

Thailand, Burma, and Laos do present a problem. But it is a problem that will have to be faced under any circumstances, regardless of whether Turkey produces opium gum or not. If the source of illegal opium can be compressed, more resources can be applied to a smaller area. This would enable the United States and the international community to concentrate its effort in Southeast Asia.

The Problem in Southeast Asia

HEROIN ADDICTION IN THE MILITARY SERVICES IN SOUTH VIETNAM

Heroine addiction in the military forces of the United States is increasing rapidly, particularly in South Vietnam, where the best estimates available are that 10 to 15 percent of all U.S. troops currently in South Vietnam are addicted to heroin in one form or another. It is estimated that in some units heroin addiction might be as high as 25 percent. Some smoke it; some sniff or "snort." From 5 to 10 percent of these inject. In the eloquent words of one concerned young American currently serving in Vietnam: *"It is ironic indeed that in the last two years of the war our biggest casualty figures will come from heroin addiction, not from combat."*

Contributing to this epidemic use of heroin is its ready availability, the frustrations and boredom growing out of the war, and the fact that the drug culture in the armed forces reflects American society as a whole. It is realistic to assume that many young Americans have used heroin prior to induction into the military services.

However, most of the addicts in South Vietnam become addicted in that country—usually within the first 30 days after entry.

Because of the quality of the heroin available in South Vietnam, it is possible to become addicted through smoking or sniffing. The "high" does not develop as quickly as when injected, but smoking or sniffing does develop a physical need for heroin. Unfortunately, most of those who smoke or sniff are under the dangerous illusion that heroin taken in this manner is not addictive. Nothing could be further from the truth.

There is also a widespread belief among many American servicemen in Vietnam that this heroin is actually cocaine, a nonaddictive drug. This, again, is not true.

Of the heroin users among the U.S. military in South Vietnam, it is estimated that 40 to 45 percent sniff, 50 percent smoke, and between 5 and 10 percent inject. Because of the purity of the heroin all are addictive, although according to medical authorities those who inject become physically dependent sooner than do those who sniff or smoke.

Those who have become addicted to the high-quality heroin available in South Vietnam will have no choice but to inject the much more diluted heroin that is available in the United States. The military services should, therefore, make every effort to detect and rehabilitate addicts before returning them to civilian society.

U.S. DEATHS FROM HEROIN ABUSE

The rate of deaths resulting from drug abuse in South Vietnam is increasing. Between August and December 1970, there were 90 deaths which were suspected to have been drug-related. Autopsy confirmed that 59 of these had died from an overdose of heroin.

In January 1971 there were 17 deaths which were

suspected to have been drug-related. In February there were 19 such deaths. Figures for March and April are not yet available, but if this trend continues, more than 200 young Americans will die of heroin addiction in 1971.

READY AVAILABILITY OF HEROIN IN SOUTH VIETNAM

Heroin is readily available to American servicemen in South Vietnam, particularly in Saigon. And it is cheap.

One-quarter gram sells for as little as $2.50 and as much as $10, while an eighth of a gram will sell for as little as $1.50 and as much as $5. Most is purchased, but a large amount is obtained by military personnel who barter cigarettes and other post exchange items for the drugs.

Contributing to the availability of heroin in Saigon is the large number of U.S. military deserters who are engaged in every form of criminal activity, including the selling of heroin.

According to figures provided by United States Army Vietnam (USARV) there are 875 such deserters, although the figure varies.

Between 400 and 500 of these live in an area of Saigon which is called Soul Alley. This area is "off limits" to U.S. personnel, and one enters at his own risk. Military police and others who have entered the area have been assaulted, robbed, stripped of their clothing and weapons, and otherwise mistreated.

United States military efforts to conduct raids into Soul Alley have failed.

The intelligence-gathering capability of the inhabitants of Soul Alley is excellent, and they are usually "tipped off" when a raid is being planned.

Nevertheless, U.S. authorities in South Vietnam should surround and raid Soul Alley and apprehend all U.S. deserters. While this would not solve the heroin problem in Vietnam, certainly it would help.

HEROIN PRODUCTION IN SOUTHEAST ASIA

Virtually all of the heroin being used by United States military personnel in South Vietnam, and an increasing amount of the heroin entering the United States, is produced from poppies grown in the remote mountain areas of Burma, Laos, Thailand, and parts of Yünnan province in Communist China.

Unfortunately, no government exercises effective administrative or political control over these areas.

Poppies are grown in areas occupied by hill tribesmen who have been growing poppies for centuries. Some of the areas of Laos and Thailand are infested with Communist guerrillas, if not actually controlled by them, while rebel bands and remnants of the Koumintang inhabit the poppy-producing areas in Burma and Thailand.

Burma, Laos, and Thailand produce an estimated 1,000 tons of raw opium, or more than one half of the world illicit output. Most of this is consumed in the Far East and Southeast Asia. Practically all observers are agreed that the largest group of users and addicts consists of overseas Chinese. Burma, Laos, and Thailand may together account for three quarters of a million users and addicts, with Burma having the largest share. Hong Kong may account for another 150,000.

Two different types of heroin are produced from the poppies grown in this area—white and purple. There is little or no indigenous requirement for white heroin in Southeast Asia—purple heroin is smoked there.

The production of white heroin in quantity is a comparatively recent development. There are no reliable statistics available to indicate what proportion of opium production is processed into heroin, but it must be concluded that production is increasing in direct proportion to the growing demand among Americans in South Vietnam.

THE MAJOR FLOW OF ILLEGAL TRAFFIC

The major flow of the traffic from the producing areas of Burma, Laos, and Thailand is directed through the Meking River Valley in the latter two countries. Major cities in these two countries, such as Luang Prabang, Vientiane, and Bangkok, serve as final markets, heroin-processing centers, and transshipment points, principally to South Vietnam and Hong Kong.

The first major collections of the raw opium in Burma are made by Koumintang irregulars and guerrilla armies of the Shan tribal insurgents who themselves convoy the product southward for delivery to wholesale operators in the cities. The latter arrange for conversion to heroin and for the domestic and export distribution of both opium and heroin. Often these wholsalers are prominent local businessmen.

In Laos, government armed forces are major wholesalers of opium and heroin and have been directly involved in large-scale smuggling activities.

The major conduit, however, is Thailand.

From the American viewpoint, Thailand is as important to the control of the illegal international traffic in narcotics as Turkey. While all of the opium produced in Southeast Asia is not grown in Thailand, most of it is smuggled through that country. Some of this is processed into heroin which is smuggled to the United States by couriers on commercial or military aircraft. Some is mailed to the United States by U.S. military personnel using both commercial and military postal services. Most, however, is smuggled into South Vietnam through both Laos and Thailand.

Recently American citizens, mostly ex-military, have moved to Thailand and have entered the business of smuggling heroin to the United States.

According to U.S. narcotics agents, the Bangkok operation is led by an ex-U.S. serviceman, William Henry Jackson. Jackson operates a place called the Five Star Bar in Bangkok, which is patronized chiefly by black U.S. servicemen. According to the narcotics agents, Jackson is assisted by other ex-military men, some of whom have moved from Europe to Bangkok. According to the agents, the Jackson group recruits patrons of the Five Star Bar as heroin couriers to the United States and utilizes other active-duty military personnel to ship heroin to the United States through the Army and Air Force Postal System.[2]

[2] The Bureau of Customs announced on May 6 that it made 248 seizures of narcotics through Army and Air Force post offices from the beginning of March through April 24, 1971. It also announced that it had seized 17 pounds of heroin in a piece of military mail from Bangkok, Thailand, on April 5. The package, seized at Fort Monmouth, New Jersey, contained heroin valued at an estimated $1.75 million on the street.

Jackson is now wanted in the United States in connection with a heroin seizure case, and American authorities are working with the Thai government to have him deported.

BNDD agents in Bangkok are of the opinion that Jackson is probably paying a Thai legislator for protection.

Bangkok is also the source of heroin for another major system engaged in smuggling heroin into the United States—the Okinawa system. This system is composed of U.S. military and ex-military personnel allied with a few Okinawans. Efforts to contain this system are hampered by the inability of authorities on Okinawa to initiate adequate customs procedures at the civilian airports. Most U.S. authorities are convinced that this will change once Okinawa reverts to Japan and Japanese law enforcement officials assume customs responsibility for Okinawa.

These Americans who are engaged in this most despicable crime of modern times carry U.S. passports with all of the privileges attendant. They are enemies of the American people, they do not deserve the rights accorded to law-abiding citizens, and serious consideration should be given to withdrawing the passports of these international criminals.

Above all, the United States government should inform the Thai government that a refusal to deport known U.S. heroin traffickers could prejudice Thai-American relations.

SMUGGLING INTO SOUTH VIETNAM

Heroin is smuggled into South Vietnam in a variety of ways. Some is carried in commercial aircraft; some is air-landed or air-dropped. Some is probably carried overland by North Vietnamese or Vietcong using trail areas used for transporting supplies, and some is carried in South Vietnamese vehicles and aircraft.

It is believed that the Laotian and South Vietnamese air forces are deeply involved in this activity. Heroin has also been smuggled in Air America aircraft, although there is no evidence that any official of a U.S. agency has ever been involved in the smuggling of heroin into South Vietnam.

It is also possible to rent private aircraft in Southeast Asia, and the use of private aircraft for smuggling purposes is increasing.

It is assumed by the U.S. military that this activity reaches high levels of command, to include the politicians, both in Laos and in South Vietnam. We were told that there is information available that high-ranking Vietnamese officials, including military, are mixed up in drug operations.

Heroin is smuggled into South Vietnam from Bangkok either by Thai soldiers returning from leave or by those beginning a tour of duty in South Vietnam. Many of these soldiers travel in U.S. military aircraft. Unfortunately, there are no adequate customs procedures in effect, and the Thai soldier enters South Vietnam unchecked. Some heroin is also carried in Thai aircraft, both military and commercial, and some is thought to be mailed by Thai military personnel through the postal system which the United States operates for the Thai military serving in Vietnam. As one American official told us, "This is an ideal situation for shipping heroin to Vietnam." Finally, some heroin is thought to be carried in by American military personnel returning from R & R. Recent evidence indicates that Hong Kong may be a limited source of the heroin reaching U.S. troops in South Vietnam.

Once the heroin reaches South Vietnam from these various sources, it becomes readily available in the streets of Saigon. The street peddler who sells heroin is the low man on the totem pole. The structure of the illegal heroin market can be illustrated as a pyramid consisting of four tiers:

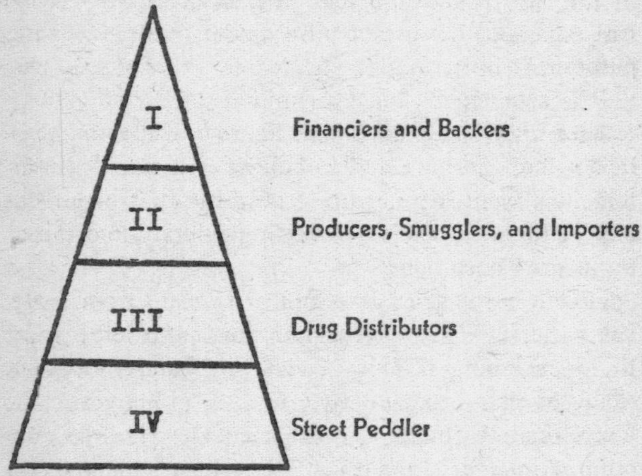

If the financiers and backers who finance the narcotics business can be uncovered and prosecuted, severe damage could be inflicted on the entire operation, especially if strong measures are taken to deal with the bottom three tiers of the pyramid simultaneously.

THE PROBLEM OF CORRUPTION

Official corruption plays an important part in the worldwide traffic in heroin. The extent of corruption in Southeast Asia is difficult to assess. Reliable sources report that at least two high-ranking Laotian officials, military and governmental, including the chief of the Laotion general staff, are deeply involved in the heroin business.

In Thailand, a former diplomat and member of one of the most respected Thai families is reputed to be one of the key figures in the opium, morphine base, and heroin operations in that country and throughout Southeast Asia.

Recently, a member of the South Vietnamese legislature, and friend of high-ranking governmental officials, was arrested smuggling heroin into Vietnam. The U.S. Military Command has supplied Ambassador Bunker with the names of high-ranking Vietnamese officials it suspects of involvement in the heroin trade, and believes that the corruption has reached the point where only forceful intervention by President Thieu can succeed in checking the traffic.

There have also been reports that Vice President Ky is implicated in the current heroin traffic. The study mission was unable to find any evidence to support this allegation.

In general the wholesale organizations trading in opium and opiates seek to involve government officials in their activities by corruption. Essentially, the wholesalers want both legal protection for themselves and insurance for the dependability of their business operations. In order to provide deliveries of contraband in large volumes and with regularity, the wholesalers seek to corrupt officialdom at fairly high levels if possible. At the same time, officialdom itself may be vulnerable to corruption because of the relatively large compensation it can get for collaborating with the major traders. For this reason, some officials are undoubtedly involved in illegal narcotics traffic.

The involvement in the traffic of individual officials and military officers in some other countries has also been reliably reported, as has the use of diplomatic pouches for smuggling opium and heroin. In no country, however, is there likely to be a flourishing illicit trade in opium or heroin without the complicity of at least a few key civil servants or police officers.

WHAT THE GOVERNMENTS OF SOUTHEAST ASIA ARE DOING

SOUTH VIETNAM

Most of the heroin in Southeast Asia is produced for Americans. Until recently this led many governments to look upon heroin usage as strictly an American problem, and little was done to help stop the illegal traffic. Addiction, however, is being discovered among the indigenous population, and the various governments are responding to U.S. initiatives in order to begin to get some control over this problem.

This is particularly true in the South Vietnamese military forces. We were told that during the South Vietnamese invasion of Laos, some South Vietnamese troops had been transferred from other areas of Vietnam on short notice had to be treated for withdrawal symptoms. Some U.S. personnel supporting the operation were also treated for withdrawal pains. The theory is that these troops were moved so rapidly and on such short notice that it was not possible to obtain sufficient heroin to satisfy their needs. As a result, one high-ranking South Vietnamese official told the study mission that whereas he had formerly looked upon the drug problem as an American problem, he now realized that it was becoming a Vietnamese problem.

Proper enforcement of South Vietnamese law would put a stop to a large part of the illegal traffic in heroin in that country. Particular emphasis must be placed on ending corruption in the customs service, which has been responsible for large quantities of heroin entering South Vietnam.

The possession of and the sale of heroin in South Vietnam is illegal. Yet sales on the streets of Saigon are so blatant that several attempts were made to sell heroin to members of the study mission as they walked the streets of Saigon, accompanied by a uniformed member of the United States Army.

As a result of American pressure the national police are becoming more aware of the need to do something about this problem. The national police commander has promised to take action.

In this context, combined narcotics suppression committees have been established in each military region. The membership consists of two U.S. officers and two inspectors from the national police. The committee collects and evaluates information on narcotics smuggling and informs the national police agencies of the need to take action to arrest and prosecute offenders.

It is too early to measure the effectiveness of these committees. In spite of the fact that heroin addiction has been a growing problem for more than a year, the committees were not established until February 1971.

The study mission was assured by U.S. Ambassador Ellsworth Bunker that both President Thieu and Vice President Ky were concerned with the problem and are interested in stopping the illegal traffic in heroin.

Promises and interest are not enough, however. Strong action must be taken to stop the heroin traffic in South Vietnam. We are not optimistic that the government is either willing or able to take such action.

One of the major reasons for pessimism is the internal political situation in South Vietnam, where differences between President Thieu and Vice President Ky inhibit effective action being taken.

Vice President Ky was especially critical of the efforts being taken by the government of South Vietnam to solve the problem of heroin, and stated that if he were given the responsibility of cleaning up "the drug mess" in South Vietnam, he would produce concrete results within two or three months.

The implication of this statement is that the government is not doing all that it can, or should. Some way must be found to convince the South Vietnamese of the urgency of this problem and the absolute necessity to solve it.

In the final analysis, neither South Vietnam nor the United States can solve this problem alone. Both need the cooperation of the producing countries: Burma, Laos, and Thailand. Of the three, Thailand is the most important, and the most able to take action.

THAILAND

According to United States officials in Bangkok, the Thai government is taking some action to stem illicit heroin production.

Since producing opium is illegal in Thailand, there are projects aimed at encouraging the hill tribesmen to grow other crops. These programs consist of education and training in new farming techniques and improved enforcement of Thai law.

The study mission visited a tribal research center which is situated on the grounds of Chiang Mai University in northern Thailand. The research center is the research branch of the Hill Tribe Division, Department of Public Welfare, Ministry of the Interior. One of the problems which led to the creation of the research center was the illegal cultivation of poppies in northern Thailand. The government was desirous of eliminating the growing of poppies, yet the economy of some of the hill societies is based upon the income derived from opium sales. Prohibition, without the promotion of alternative cash crops, would have caused considerable hardships. In addition, the inability of the government to exert effective administrative control over these areas would have doomed the project to failure.

In 1967 and again in 1970, the Thai government requested the United Nations to help by conducting a study on the economic and social needs of the opium-producing areas in Thailand.

There have also been efforts to resettle the hill tribes to other areas, but this program has not been overly successful.

The Thai government has initiated efforts to destroy the poppy crops, but without great success. The areas are too remote and enforcement almost impossible because of the Communist-inspired insurgency in the area.

In 1962, the Thai invited U.S. BNDD agents into Thailand to assist them in their efforts. Relations between BNDD agents and the Thai police are improving. The Thai now permit BNDD agents to operate undercover and to appear in court in narcotics cases.

BNDD efforts, at least until 1969, were hampered because funds needed to do an effective job were not available. This situation has also changed, and sufficient funds are now being made available.

Much more cooperation on the part of the Thai government is required, however. The Thai must devote more resources to improvement of their capability to intercept illegal shipments of opium, morphine, and heroin.

The Thai government must also institute adequate and effective customs inspection, especially in the case of Thai troops and aircraft going to and from South Vietnam.

The study mission was also of the opinion that the United States Mission in Thailand should be more forceful in convincing the Thai government that the United States not only needs, but expects, rapidly increasing action to stop the illegal traffic in opium and its derivatives.

Strong and effective measures by the Thai government, however, would not completely solve the problem. Poppies are also grown in Burma and Laos.

BURMA

Poppies are grown in Burma under uncontrolled conditions. Owing to economic, social, and political factors, the government is not able to apply control measures required to implement their policies or intentions of prohibiting, or to supervise and control the growing of, poppies and the production of opium. While much of the opium produced in Burma is consumed locally, a considerable amount appears in the illicit traffic. It is bartered for goods or sold for cash. Opium is very often the principal cash crop.

Burma has few economic, political, or cultural contacts with the outside world as a result of the government's acute sensitivity to foreign influence. Because of this, U.S. relations with Burma are not close, although they are "correct and friendly."

Any reduction in the amount of opium produced in Burma will take time. The government must be strengthened and some way found to convince the opium producers to grow other crops.

There is little that the United States can do unilaterally to bring this about. It can, and must, however, urge the United Nations to help.

LAOS

The Laotians are deeply involved in the growing of poppies and in the production of heroin. Opium is the principal source of income of the ethnic minorities in Laos.

The possession of opium in Laos is not illegal at the present time. There is a law being considered which would make such possession illegal. Even if the law passes, enforcement will be next to impossible because of the inability of the Laotian government to exercise effective political control over most of Laos. . . .

There are other steps that the Laotians can take to assert some control over the illegal traffic in opium and its derivatives. From the evidence available, there is no doubt that the Laotian military is deeply involved in the international traffic in heroin. Heroin is processed in laboratories located in Laos, and what is not smuggled through Thailand is smuggled through Laos, primarily by air in Laotian Air Force planes. While there is little likelihood that the Laotian government will gain control over its territory in the near future, it can, and must, take action to reform its air force and eliminate the corruption which permits the drug traffic to flourish.

It should also be pointed out that tribesmen who grow poppies in the non-Communist part of Laos are some of the most effective resistance fighters against the North Vietnamese and the Pathet Lao. They depend for their livelihood upon opium production. The United States should consider the feasibility of buying up the opium crop each year, while encouraging and assisting the tribesmen to grow other crops. Such a program would probably cost at the most $10 million annually. In five years, however, it would not equal the amount of military assistance that the United States gives to Laos annually to enable it to remain non-Communist. If it is in the national security interests of the United States to save three million Laotians from communism, it certainly is in the national security interest of the United States to spend whatever is necessary to save generations of young Americans from heroin addiction.

In summary, the heroin problem in Southeast Asia is a regional problem. It transcends national boundaries, and the operations in one country are dependent upon the operations in the other. Efforts to combat it must, therefore, be regional in scope. And the United States must push the fight against heroin as vigorously as it has conducted the fight against Communist aggression in Southeast Asia.

For years the United States has been encouraging regional economic development in Southeast Asia. It is discouraging that the most successful regional commercial development has been the illicit production and sale of heroin.

WHAT THE UNITED STATES IS DOING TO ATTACK THE HEROIN PROBLEM IN SOUTH VIETNAM

Steps are being taken by the United States government in South Vietnam at both the diplomatic level and the military level to combat the growing heroin problem.

The study mission learned that the United States has made a strong appeal to the government of South Vietnam to take action in this area. In a strongly worded memorandum, the U.S. ambassador pointed out that "continuation of illegal traffic in drugs, particularly heroin, will have a serious impact on American support of the national effort."

Because there has been criticism of U.S. diplomats for not pressing the narcotics issue forcefully enough with host governments, it is only fair to say that the study mission wholeheartedly supports the efforts of the embassy in South Vietnam. Following is an extract from the paper:

DRUG ABUSE

GOALS

Accordingly it is suggested that the following goals be established:

1. Recognition by all Vietnamese officials and citizens of the magnitude of the drug problem and the serious impact that a continuation of illicit traffic in drugs, particularly heroin, will have on the American support of the national effort.
2. Development of a national will to eradicate trafficking in drugs.

RECOMMENDATIONS

To achieve these goals it is specifically recommended that the President of Vietnam:

1. Issue a circular in the immediate future, through both civilian and military components of the government, indicating your concern over the accelerating drug problem and the apparent involvement of large numbers of Vietnamese in drug trafficking. This circular should specifically mention the trafficking of heroin and the danger this highly addictive narcotic currently poses to the physical well-being of Americans as well as the future danger it poses to Vietnamese citizens. This circular should be followed by a decree which specifically legislates against trafficking in heroin and which imposes severe penalties for doing so.
2. Appoint a Presidential Task Force of highly qualified, dedicated and honest investigators to ferret out, investigate and prosecute the financiers and backers who comprise the powers behind drug trafficking. These men are responsible for manipulating, fostering, protecting and promoting the illicit traffic in drugs. They include

influential political figures, government officials and moneyed ethnic Chinese members of the criminal syndicate now flourishing in the Cholon sector of Saigon.
3. Initiate action to establish a comprehensive drug training program for all law enforcement elements within the Republic of Vietnam, to include prosecutors. Such training would be directed primarily at heroin, its characteristics and the danger it poses to the physical well-being of users.
4. Initiate immediate action to arrest all importers, distributors and street peddlers involved in the distribution and sale of drugs, especially heroin. Further, that stringent penalties be levied against these people to preclude their return to these activities.
5. Initiate action to form a specialized narcotics section within the Customs Fraud Repression Service. Such a section would devote its energy to combat the smuggling of drugs, especially heroin.
6. Take immediate action to have existing customs regulations enforced. Specific actions that must be taken are:
(*a*) Unauthorized personnel must not be allowed to handle any items of cargo or baggage until such items have been properly cleared by customs officials.
(*b*) Existing customs regulations pertaining to the actual processing and searching of individuals and all classes of cargo/personnel must be adhered to rigidly.
7. Initiate action to enforce existing health and welfare laws as they pertain to the sale of pharmaceutical products (dangerous drugs) throughout Vietnam. No such products should be sold to American servicemen without the required prescription.

U.S. military authorities in South Vietnam are also aware that the problem of heroin addiction has reached epidemic proportions and must be solved. To do this, a four-point program has been developed, consisting of education, amnesty, rehabilitation, and suppression.

Education programs have been expanded at all levels

of command where the consequences of drug abuse are stressed. There are also programs aimed at educating noncommissioned and commissioned officers in the detection and control of drug abuse in their units.

An education program to be effective must stress the dangers inherent in the illegal use of drugs and the dangers it poses to the health and future of the user. It must be current, accurate, and hard-hitting.

There has been criticism that material provided for use in Vietnam does not fit these requirements. According to one recognized authority, more use should be made of films which "tell it like it is." These films should be kept up to date and they should focus on the problem in South Vietnam.

Amnesty programs have been instituted. Basically, amnesty is a promise of freedom from punishment in exchange for accepting medical treatment and rehabilitation. Under this program, when an addict requests rehabilitation treatment and medical assistance, he is admitted to a rehabilitation center, where he undergoes treatment for his addiction. To prevent the amnesty program from being used as a vehicle to escape from combat and to discourage resumption of the habit, an individual is permitted to request amnesty only one time.

While there has been no success in curing those who inject, there have been some successes in curing those who sniff or smoke. There are very few statistics available concerning rehabilitation programs. They must, therefore, be used with caution.

For example, during the first quarter of 1971, 3,458 heroin users participated in the rehabilitation program. Of this number, there were at least 703 known unsuccessful participants. There are no figures available which estimate the rate of cure of those participating. From statistics that are available, the rate of cure is not encouraging. For instance, of 532 addicts treated at Pioneer House, an amnesty and rehabilitation center located in Long Binh, between October 1970 and March 1971, there were reported 149 successful cures, 94 failures, and 249 in the unsure category.

An important part of the rehabilitation program is the counseling received during the treatment period. Even here, the program is vulnerable. For instance, the week before the study mission visited Long Binh, two counselors at Pioneer House were arrested, one for using LSD, the other for using heroin.

Another problem emanates from the requirement that the amnesty and rehabilitation program is entirely voluntary. The individual is free to leave the center at any time. In the past, people have walked out of the rehabilitation center before they were cured. They will probably do the same in the future.

But perhaps the most serious shortcoming of the drug rehabilitation program is that there is not a coordinated Vietnam-wide effort to establish rehabilitation centers. Responsibility is delegated to major commanders. Some commands support the effort fully. Some distrust the concept and take little or no interest in the program.

Several steps have also been taken to suppress the use of drugs, particularly heroin, in South Vietnam. Drug-abuse councils have been formed in every unit down to battalion/squadron level to provide analysis, evaluation, and monitoring of all aspects of narcotics and drug suppression. A combined antinarcotics enforcement committee, composed of Vietnamese and American forces, has also been established in each military region to eliminate the illicit traffic in narcotics within the civilian community of the Republic of Vietnam.

In addition, a Joint United States/Republic of Vietnam Narcotics Investigative Detachment will concentrate its efforts on the illegal drug supply and trafficking problem to interdict and eradicate drug sources before the heroin reaches military personnel. This detachment is made up of representatives from the several U.S. military investigative organizations, the Vietnamese Military Police, and the Vietnamese National Police.

Simultaneously, a Joint U.S. Customs Group has been established to assume responsibility for all military customs operations in Vietnam to include postal, household goods, unaccompanied baggage, and the processing of accompanied baggage and personnel arriving or departing South Vietnam. This unit is responsible for all customs enforcement, including narcotics.

Hopefully, these steps will help reduce the availability and use of heroin by U.S. personnel in South Vietnam.

There is one other aspect of the problem which is of concern to military authorities in South Vietnam—they have no adequate and reliable procedures for detecting the heroin addict. As part of the drug-suppression program, new and more complete surveying techniques are to be employed, and statistical data will be collected and compiled on a commandwide basis.

Measures must be taken to improve the reliability of addict detection procedures. If possible, the development of a simplified urinalysis test should become a matter of first priority for medical authorities. If this is not feasible, adequate laboratory facilities should be furnished down to battalion and squadron level. Every soldier should be required to undergo periodic urinalysis, especially before his return to the United States and absolutely before his separation from the military service. If the serviceman who has become addicted using 94 to 97 percent pure heroin in South Vietnam enters the drug scene in the United States, where the heroin available is 4 to 6 percent pure, the ominous implications are obvious for himself, his family, and American society. In the absence of the heroin available in South Vietnam, the only alternative for one who has become addicted through sniffing and snorting will be to inject.

Implementation of the above program must receive the highest priority at every level of command, and it must be pushed with a greater sense of urgency than has been the case. In spite of the fact that drug abuse has been a growing problem in South Vietnam for more than a year, the directive setting out the program to combat it was not issued until December 1970.

While U.S. military and diplomatic personnel in Southeast Asia are concerned about the problem, the study mission is of the opinion that a greater sense of urgency is needed.

For example, when we arrived in Bangkok, we were told that there was a regional conference being held to discuss the problem of drug addiction among U.S. military personnel in Southeast Asia. All U.S. agencies responsible for the drug problem were represented at the meeting. This included the military, the Bureau of Customs, the Bureau of Narcotics and Dangerous Drugs, and U.S. diplomatic personnel.

While it was encouraging to note that this conference was finally held, such action should have been taken much sooner to mobilize the resources available to take strong coordinated action to stop the illegal traffic in heroin.

Iran and Japan

The study mission also traveled to Iran and Japan in an effort to determine what impact, if any, those countries had upon the heroin problem in the United States. We are happy to report that there is no evidence to suggest that either contributes in any way to the illegal production and smuggling of heroin into the United States.

What was of particular interest to us was the approach that the two countries have taken, and are taking, to control heroin addiction.

In both, these procedures are aimed at suppression of the illegal traffic, rehabilitation of the addicts when found, and strict justice for those convicted for illegal possession of, or trafficking in, heroin.

IRAN

Iran has one of the largest heroin-using populations in the world—approximately 50,000. Unlike the United States, 90 percent of the heroin used in Iran is produced illegally in that country. The remaining 10 percent required by the Iranian heroin addict population originates in the poppy fields of Turkey.

In 1955, because opium addiction was undermining

the health of the nation, Iran banned the growing of poppies.

By 1969, discouraged by the lack of movement on the part of Turkey and Afghanistan, and alarmed by the gold drain which covered the cost of illicitly imported opium, Iran authorized limited poppy cultivation under strictly controlled conditions.

Iran has strict opium collection procedures and the poppy crop is closely monitored from planting until the harvest of the opium gum. And whereas the government of Turkey pays the farmer $10 to $15 for opium gum, the government of Iran pays $90. This, of course, explains in part why there is little or no leakage of opium gum from the licit to the illicit market in Iran.

There are other reasons. If the farmer in Iran violates the law, he forfeits his license to grow poppies. And if an individual in Iran is convicted of possession or trafficking in heroin, he is executed. (Since 1969, 86 people have been shot for offenses involving heroin.)

In the past, Turkish smugglers moved raw opium into Iran. As a result of strict enforcement of Iranian narcotics legislation and efforts by both Turkish and Iranian governments to combat smuggling, the amount of opium introduced from Turkey has been reduced dramatically. Now, however, instead of smuggling raw opium, the Turks are smuggling morphine base and heroin. This is a new development.

It is easier to deal in morphine gum or heroin which has one-tenth the bulk of opium gum. In addition, opium gum has a distinctive odor and in hot weather is extremely difficult to conceal, while morphine base or heroin is almost odorless.

This poses a potential problem of severe dimensions for the entire international effort to control the illegal traffic in narcotics.

The evidence suggests that the drug traffickers in the Marseilles area of France are becoming concerned at the increasing pressure being applied by the French authorities in cooperation with U.S. Bureau of Narcotics and Dangerous Drug agents. It is thought that they may be looking for other areas in which to operate their illicit laboratories. If heroin is produced in Turkey, at the source of the opium gum, it will remove the necessity to smuggle opium gum or morphine base to France. The long, circuitous route from Turkey to Marseilles provides an opportunity for law enforcement agencies to intercept the shipment at any step along the way and particularly in Marseilles, where it is halted long enough to be turned into heroin. If, on the other hand, heroin production takes place in Turkey on a scale large enough to provide the illegal heroin formerly produced in Marseilles, interception will become much more difficult.

It is obvious that Turkey must introduce effective opium production controls and work toward a complete abolition of opium production. The heroin problem in Iran and the United States is fueled by the opium that originates in Turkey, and it is that country that can do the most toward helping to solve the heroin addiction problem.

JAPAN

The Japanese have been able to control heroin addiction. Since 1964 they have succeeded in reducing their heroin addict population from approximately 50,-000 to only several thousand.

The success of Japanese efforts to control addiction is due to effective Japanese police work and to strict penalties dealing with the narcotics pusher.

The maximum penalty is 10 years in prison for smuggling or selling heroin.

If a man is arrested for heroin pushing, there is no bail permitted. He must be charged within 48 hours, however. The police can hold the suspect for 10 days, during which preindictment investigations are conducted. At the end of 10 days, he is turned over to the prosecutor, who has an additional 10 days to bring the accused to trial. If necessary, the prosecutor can request an additional 10 days before commencing trial. Therefore, an individual arrested for possession of heroin can be held for 30 days without bail.

It is the opinion of the study mission that law enforcement officials and legislators in the United States should study the methods used by Japan to deal with this problem.

International Cooperation to Control Illegal Heroin Traffic

It is obvious that if the illegal traffic in heroin is to be brought under control, international cooperation is needed. The most immediate problem is to control the cultivation of poppies and the production of opium.

The production of legal opium is regulated by the International Narcotics Control Board (INCB) through the provisions of the Single Convention of 1961, which became internationally effective December 13, 1964.

The Board is entrusted with enforcing the provisions of the Single Convention. The Board asks both parties and nonparties to the Convention for estimates of drug requirements and existing stocks and statistics of production, consumption, and seizures each year, and by article 12(3), if estimates are not forthcoming, the Board can fix them. Among the weapons which the Board has are requests for information and explanations, public declarations that a country has violated its obligations, and under article 14(2), a recommendation to parties that they impose embargoes on imports and exports against an offending country.

Member states are also required to license the growing of poppies and to control trade by granting export licenses only when the importer produces an import certificate from the importing country. A third country is not to allow drugs to pass through its territory without a copy of the export authorization.

The provisions of the Single Convention, however, apply only to the control of legal production of opium. They provide essentially voluntary restraints on parties with respect to cultivation of the opium poppy, production of opium, manufacture of opium-derived drugs, and import and export of these substances. The United States has proposed amendments which, if adopted, would provide the INCB with authority to control production and illegal traffic in narcotic drugs.

It is hoped that a conference to consider the proposed amendments would meet early in 1972.

While the study mission fully supports U.S. efforts to strengthen the ability of the international community to restrict narcotics activity to legitimate medical and scientific purposes, it is of the opinion that such a conference should be convened as soon as possible and not wait until early in 1972. Time is essential and the United States should impress this fact on the international community at every opportunity.

The problem, however, is not the control of legal production, but to find ways to stop leakage of opium to the illegal market. Some countries such as India, Iran, the Soviet Union, and Yugoslavia have been relatively successful in accomplishing this. Others such as Turkey have not.

Complicating the problem are those areas of Afghanistan, Pakistan, Burma, Laos, and Thailand where opium poppies are grown illegally and under uncontrolled conditions.

Because of the amount and quality of heroin produced from the poppies grown in Burma, Laos, Thailand, and Turkey, international efforts to control the illegal traffic in heroin must be concentrated on those four countries.

Experience has demonstrated that the only way to control this problem is to control it at the source—in the poppy fields.

The United States can, and should, exercise what bilateral diplomatic and economic pressures it can to encourage its friends and allies to take action to stop opium production. It is also necessary to obtain the cooperation of the United Nations.

Acting upon the initiative of the United States the United Nations did agree to establish a Special Fund for Drug Abuse Controls, to be made up of voluntary contributions and used to develop short-term and long-term plans and programs to bring the problem of drug addiction under control.

The United States pledged $2 million and on April 1, 1971, the permanent U.S. representative to the United Nations made the first $1 million payment. Unfortunately, the United States is the only country to have pledged any money, although one other, West Germany, has announced unofficially that it will pay approximately $350,000 into the fund.

This is disappointing. With addiction increasing around the world, particularly in the United States, there is an immediate need for effective action and co-operation.

According to the Secretary General, the purpose of the drug abuse fund will be to develop short-term and long-term plans and programs and to provide assistance in the execution of those plans and programs. During the initial stages of the Fund, pending the completion and submission of a proposed long-term policy and plan of action which would deal with al laspects of the problems related to drug abuse control, the voluntary contributions to the Fund will be used for specific projects to be included in a short-term program without prejudice to on-going projects. The short-term program will consist of projects to expand the research and information facilities of United Nations drug control bodies; to plan and implement programs of technical assistance in pilot projects for crop substitution purposes, the establishment and improvement of national drug control administrations and enforcement machinery, and training of personnel, and in setting up or expanding research and training centers which could serve national or regional needs; to enlarge the capabilities and extend the operations of United Nations drug control bodies and their secretariats; to promote facilities for the treatment, rehabilitation, and social reintegration of drug addicts; and to develop educational material and programs suitable for use on high-risk populations.

While this is a commendable program and should be encouraged, it does not go to the heart of the problem—how to stop the illegal traffic in heroin now; or how to get Turkey to honor her international treaty obligations by passing a law licensing the growing of poppies; or what is to be done to control the growing of poppies and the production and smuggling of heroin in the Far East.

These are the basic problems, and, if necessary, the United States should be willing to make funds available to the United Nations, or to the individual countries, so that they might begin to deal with them.

The United States also must convince the world community of the urgency of this problem.

INTERNATIONAL CRIMINAL POLICE ORGANIZATION (INTERPOL)

Essentially, the purpose of Interpol is to enable police forces in the different countries to coordinate their work effectively in the double aim of law enforcement and crime prevention.

Interpol is not an enforcement body, nor is it an investigating body. It collects, collates, stores, and disseminates information on known international criminals.

It has a staff of 107, of which 12 devote full time to narcotics matters.

Interpol is hampered in its efforts to assist in the control of narcotics by:

1. bad communications between police units in the member countries;
2. corruption in the police units or on a higher national level; and
3. poor administrative and police control over large parts of the country, such as in Thailand, Laos, and Burma.

Another problem is that Interpol does not receive a great amount of intelligence from member countries concerning the smuggling of narcotics. If a foreign national is arrested for a narcotics offense, the national police are required to provide Interpol with all of the information surrounding the case. This is not always done. Until January 1971 one of the greatest offenders was the United States.

The United States is also currently behind in its dues to Interpol. The dues were increased in 1969 from $28,500 per year to $48,780. The United States needed legislative authority to pay the difference—authority which has not yet been granted.

There have been a number of suggestions made that Interpol could increase its effectiveness by improving its communications facilities and by computerizing its operations. The Study mission discussed this with Interpol officials at some length. Although it was the considered opinion of those experts that such improvements would make Interpol operations more efficient, they pointed out that there were no funds available for this: Interpol operates on an annual budget of less than $1 million and any additional equipment would require an increase in the annual dues.

It has been suggested that the United States should make money available to Interpol to introduce these modernization programs. This could be done, but it should be done with caution and in such a way as to preclude the assumption that the United States is trying to "take over" Interpol.

The United States should consider ways to improve the communications capabilities of Interpol and the member countries, either on a bilateral basis or through the Interpol apparatus.

OTHER INTERNATIONAL ORGANIZATIONS

In addition to action in the United Nations and increased cooperation with Interpol, the United States should also consider putting pressure on our allies in the North Atlantic Treaty Organization (NATO) and the Southeast Asia Treaty Organization (SEATO). Both are mutual security treaties, and both pledge action against a common foe. Heroin addiction is an enemy of mankind, and all the world's resources should be mobilized against it.

The United States furnishes approximately $100 million military assistance to Turkey annually to enable that country to fulfill her commitment to the North Atlantic Treaty Organization (NATO). NATO was organized to protect the security of the North Atlantic area, including the United States. During the 22 years that NATO has been in existence, the United States has contributed well over $20 billion to ensure its survival. Money is no object when it comes to the defense of the free world. The U.S. defense budget in 1971 will be approximately $79 billion, plus another $2 billion for military assistance.

But how well will we have defended America, if we lose a generation of young Americans to heroin addiction in the process?

Europe depends upon the United States for its security. It should be willing to do what is necessary to help solve this problem, including putting pressure on Turkey to take effective action to first control and then to stop the growing of poppies.

The same situation applies in Southeast Asia. Thailand is a SEATO partner, and Laos and South Vietnam fall under the U.S. security blanket. They must all be persuaded to join in the battle against heroin now.

Conclusions

1. As of May 1971, there are an estimated 250,000 heroin addicts in the United States and an additional 30,000–40,000 addicts among U.S. troops in Southeast Asia.

2. The problem is how to stop heroin from reaching American addicts in the United States and in Southeast Asia. Once the poppy is cut and introduced into illegal channels, the battle to prevent the end product, heroin, from reaching the addict is virtually lost.

3. Heroin addiction is essentially an American problem, and most countries view it as such. As a result, there is a great deal of talk about cooperation with the United States, but there is very little action.

4. There is no sense of urgency on the part of most

governments that action must be taken immediately to stop the illegal production of, and traffic in, heroin. U.S. diplomatic personnel must assign top priority to gaining the full cooperation of host governments in attempting to solve the heroin problem.

5. Turkey must stop growing opium poppies if this problem is to be brought under control. Most of the heroin entering the United States originates in the poppy fields of Turkey.

6. Prospects for stopping poppy cultivation and the production of heroin in Southeast Asia in the near future are dim. Efforts must be directed toward stopping the illegal flow of heroin into South Vietnam. If these efforts fail, the only solution is to withdraw American servicemen from Southeast Asia. Above all, the U.S. diplomatic community in the several countries must be aware that their job is to represent United States interests rather than to appease the host government.

7. The United States can and should exert pressures on the governments in Southeast Asia in order to gain their cooperation in the fight against heroin. The survival of Laos and South Vietnam depend upon continued military and economic assistance from the United States, and the ability of Thailand to defend itself would be seriously weakened if the United States were to discontinue military assistance to that country. While the effectiveness of threats to cut off military and economic assistance are debatable, there can be no disagreement that because of this assistance the United States has a right to expect full cooperation from these countries in efforts to stop illegal traffic in heroin.

8. Corruption plays an important role in the illegal heroin traffic, particularly in Southeast Asia. Govern-

mental and military officials at all levels are implicated. If graft and corruption are to be eliminated, some way must be found to take the profit out of the production and sale of heroin.

Recommendations

1. That the President take personal command of the struggle to eliminate the illegal international traffic in narcotics, particularly heroin, and commit the full resources of the country to that battle.

2. That every U.S. department and agency engaged in the conduct of foreign policy be instructed to participate in a broad-based diplomatic offensive to gain the full cooperation of foreign governments in eliminating the illegal traffic in opium and its derivatives. These instructions should require each U.S. country team to draw up a comprehensive and specific plan for gaining greater cooperation from the host government. Such plans should entail the escalating use of all available political and economic leverages, and each foreign government should be put on notice that failure to cooperate would prejudice bilateral relations. To buttress the efforts made abroad, the Department of State should undertake a concerted campaign to impress on foreign ambassadors in Washington and at the United Nations the seriousness of the U.S. government's concern.

3. That the U.S. government immediately and forcefully exercise the special leverages it has with the South Vietnamese and Royal Laotian governments by virtue

of our enormous military, economic, and political support of those governments to gain their cooperation in cracking down on the illegal heroin trade in their countries and the official corruption that contributes to it.

4. That the U.S. government underwrite an accelerated research program to find a nonaddictive substitute for opium, which continues to have important medicinal applications.

5. That the United States negotiate with other countries to better control and, where feasible, stop the cultivation of opium poppies. To help accomplish this, the United States must be prepared to undertake a multimillion-dollar bilateral program to assist those countries to develop substitute economic activities for their opium farmers.

6. That the permanent U.S. representative to the United Nations continue his initiatives to gain greater UN participation in the fight against illicit narcotics and dangerous drugs, emphasizing efforts to:

a. gain the strong support of the Secretary General in this struggle;

b. push vigorously to ensure adoption of amendments to the Single Convention which have been proposed by the United States;

c. gain participation by all nations in the UN Special Fund for Drug Abuse Control; and

d. initiate proposals designed to upgrade the capabilities of the United Nations Division on Narcotic Drugs and the International Narcotics Control Board in terms of personnel and funding. Special emphasis should be placed on the development of programs by the UN Division on Narcotic Drugs to provide alternate economic activities for opium farmers.

7. That U.S. military authorities in Southeast Asia undertake all apropriate policing measures to reduce the flow of heroin to U.S. troops in South Vietnam, including increasing the surveillance of mail entering South Vietnam through APO channels. Customs procedures must also be expanded to include inspection of Thai soldiers entering South Vietnam aboard U.S. military aircraft.

8. That the Department of Defense improve its capability to identify military heroin addicts by instituting an extensive program of urinalysis; that it provide acute care and detoxification for all military addicts; and that it provide basic rehabilitation services for those addicts. That in cases where military rehabilitation efforts prove unsuccessful, the unrehabilitated addict's commanding officer should be permitted and required, prior to the addict's discharge from the military, to civilly commit the addict to the administrator of the Veterans' Administration for a period of three years for treatment and rehabilitation. That the Veterans' Administration in turn contract with civilian multimodality treatment centers at the community level with the purposes of utilizing the centers' expertise within the VA hospitals and ultimately turning the patient over to such centers for reintegration into society.

9. That the United States substantially speed up the withdrawal of military draftees from South Vietnam. The draftees have proven far more susceptible to heroin addiction than nondraftees and are estimated to have an addiction rate of over 15 percent.

10. That the Congress consider legislation which would provide for preventive detention, in the form of a nonbailable offense, for those arrested for the illegal possession of, or trafficking in, heroin, who are not addicted themselves. This legislation should also consist of a mandatory jail sentence of not less than 20 years upon conviction with no possibility of parole.

11. That the Congress consider legislation which would ban the manufacture, distribution, sale, or possession with intent to use, drug materials for illegal purposes.

12. That the United States consider canceling the passport of any American known to be engaged in the illegal traffic in heroin.

13. That U.S. customs authorities increase the surveillance of mail entering the United States through APO channels.

14. That the United States utilize its world-wide intelligence collection aparatus, including the use of satellite photography, to gather information on all aspects of the illegal production of and traffic in heroin.

15. That substantial new funds be made available to the Bureau of Narcotics and Dangerous Drugs for discretionary expenditure.

16. That the United States consider making additional funds available to Interpol to improve its operations.

17. That the United States seek greater cooperation from the government of Switzerland to identify individuals who utilize secret Swiss bank accounts to finance the traffic in heroin.

18. That Congress extend an invitation to the Parliament of Turkey to join in the creation of an inter-

parliamentary group to consider ways and means of attacking the illegal production and sale of opium and its derivatives.

19. That the Committee on Foreign Affairs conduct an in-depth series of hearings to consider the several legislative proposals that have been made to deal with the illegal international traffic in narcotics.

REP. MORGAN MURPHY (*Dem.-Illinois*)
REP. ROBERT STEELE (*Rep.-Connecticut*)

May 1971